The Best You Can Be

To

Mari, with Love.........

1997

DOROTHY EATON WATTS

The Best
You Can
Be

A Woman's Guide
to Personal Growth

Review and Herald® Publishing Association
Hagerstown, MD 21740

The author assumes full responsibility for the accuracy of all facts and quotations as cited in this book.

Texts credited to NIV are from the *Holy Bible, New International Version*. Copyright © 1973, 1978, 1984, International Bible Society. Used by permission of Zondervan Bible Publishers.

Bible texts credited to RSV are from the Revised Standard Version of the Bible, copyright © 1946, 1952, 1971, by the Division of Christian Education of the National Council of the Churches of Christ in the U.S.A. Used by permission.

Verses marked TLB are taken from *The Living Bible*, copyright © 1971 by Tyndale House Publishers, Wheaton, Ill. Used by permission.

This book was
Edited by Richard W. Coffen
Designed by Bill Kirstein
Cover art by Patricia Wegh
Typeset: 11/13 Times Roman

PRINTED IN U.S.A.

98 97 96 95 94   10 9 8 7 6 5 4 3 2

Library of Congress Cataloging in Publication Data
Watts, Dorothy Eaton, 1937-
    The best you can be: a woman's guide to personal growth / Dorothy
Eaton Watts.
        p.   cm.
    Includes bibliographical references.
    1. Women—Religious life. 2. Spiritual life—Seventh-day
Adventists. 3. Seventh-day Adventists—Membership. I. Title.
BV4527.W37   1993
248.8'43—dc20   93-17358
                                                      CIP

ISBN 0-8280-0722-5

Dedicated

to David Ronald Watts—
my husband, mentor, and best friend.
More than anyone else he has encouraged me to be
all that God has gifted me to become.

Lord, Help Me to Become

Lord, help me to become what the world is waiting to see—
A woman who is all You have gifted her to be.

A woman possessed with a noble vision
Of what she might become in Your plan;
A woman of destiny with a holy mission;
A woman ready to say, "By God's grace I can!"

A loving woman, with peace, joy, and patience,
Revealing Your character, Your power, Your grace;
A spiritual woman, who takes time each day
To fill her cup, know Your will, seek Your face.

A woman with courage; unafraid to risk
Failure that she might gain success;
A woman ready to stretch beyond her limits
And in the striving find true happiness.

A determined woman, ready to face any test;
A woman with a purpose, who will not give in.
A woman who dares to reach, to achieve her best.
A woman of excellence! A woman who wins!

O God, make me such a woman!
A woman who is all that You have gifted her to be!

Contents

CHAPTER ONE

A Successful Woman

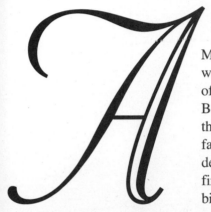MANDA SMITH was a success, a woman of excellence, an example of the kind of woman I'd like to be. Born a slave near the beginning of the nineteenth century, one of a family of 13, she lived through the deaths of several children and a first husband, as well as the instability of a second unhappy marriage.

Yet Amanda's story is one of spiritual triumph and success. Despite her circumstances she became an internationally acclaimed missionary evangelist, preaching in England, India, Africa, and other parts of the world.

One well-known individual of that time said this about Amanda Smith: "She is a Christian of the highest type, and as a simple, confiding child of God has no superior among any women of our time." A minister who knew Amanda well referred to her as "God's image carved in ebony."

Once when Amanda stood to sing before an audience of women of rank and wealth, she suddenly realized that she was only a washerwoman with but two years of education, and she began to tremble.

How can I possibly go out there and sing in front of all

those privileged women? Amanda thought. And then she remembered that her success was not to be measured in status, money, power, or position. Rather, it was to be measured in what she did with what God had given her. Her success was not to be counted by her position in the world, but by her position in Christ.

Amanda told herself, *I belong to royalty and am well acquainted with the King of kings and am better known and better understood among the great family above than I am on earth.*

She took a deep breath, walked out into the spotlight—her head held high—and praised God for all that was within her. Her concert was a success.

From that day new opportunities miraculously opened to Amanda Smith. She went through each door God opened and did her best to be all that He had gifted her to become. Amanda came that day to the place all successful women must come, the point of accepting her own self-worth. In those few moments as Amanda quaked backstage, she suddenly got a glimpse of who she really was in Christ—someone unique, created in the image of God, purchased by Jesus' death on the cross, and placed on earth to accomplish a work that no one else could do.

From the life of Amanda Smith I have learned five principles of successful living.

1. There is a difference between worldly success and godly success. In her book *The Challenge of Being a Woman* Alice Painter points out five foundations of worldly success and self-esteem: possessions, performance, position, appearance, and people. What do I have? How well do I do? How important am I? How do I look? What do people think about me? Success, then, becomes my way of proving that I am special, that I have worth and value.

True success, on the other hand, begins with that sense of worth and uniqueness which comes from our position in Christ. We are already special, created in His image, and loved with an everlasting love. Success, then, becomes a striving to be all that God has already gifted me to become. Success is reaching toward my full potential in Christ Jesus. It is finding my place in His plan.

2. *I am somebody, a child of God, created in His image.*

"The Lord hath called me from the womb; from the bowels of my mother hath he made mention of my name" (Isa. 49:1).

"For you created my inmost being; you knit me together in my mother's womb. I praise you because I am fearfully and wonderfully made; your works are wonderful, I know that full well. My frame was not hidden from you when I was made in the secret place. When I was woven together in the depths of the earth, your eyes saw my unformed body. All the days ordained for me were written in your book before one of them came to be" (Ps. 139:13-16, NIV).

How unique I am! I was not made in Korea. There is no "Made in Brazil" label on me. I was fashioned in the darkness of my mother's womb by God's hand, created for a purpose, destined to walk onto the stage of the universe at this hour of earth's history. Success is discovering that plan and coming into harmony with it.

Amazing thought! While I was still but a microscopic cell, God arranged my DNA and lined up my genes and chromosomes to make me the special person that I am. There is none other like me among the 6 billion people living on Planet Earth. No one else has my distinct thumbprint, my distinct voiceprint, my special looks, my combination of gifts and personality.

If this is true, then what if I have a genetic disorder? Did God not know that when I was being formed, and does He not plan for my success, giving me a special work that He wants me to do in spite of my handicap? What if I find schoolwork difficult or have a shy temperament? Can He not work all things together for good, as He has promised in Romans 8:28?

3. *Jesus died to assure my success.* Because of the death

of Christ on Calvary the wealth of the universe is mine. I am now a child of the King, a daughter of God. Not only do I have forgiveness for past mistakes, acceptance despite my blunders, but I have the power of Heaven on my side to assure my success. Through Christ I have direct access to the throne of God and the promise of angels to help me in my endeavors.

"I can do all things through Christ which strengtheneth me" (Phil. 4:13).

"Thou shalt have good success. . . . Be strong and of a good courage; be not afraid, neither be thou dismayed: for the Lord thy God is with thee whithersoever thou goest" (Joshua 1:8, 9).

Success is one of the 3,573 promises of God's Word that I can claim. I can ask for success, knowing that God will keep His word and give me what He has promised. If I ask Him, He will make me a successful woman!

4. God has a special plan for my life. "Not more surely is the place prepared for us in the heavenly mansions than is the special place designated on earth where we are to work for God" (Ellen G. White, *Christ's Object Lessons*, p. 327).

"Arise, shine; for thy light is come, and the glory of the Lord is risen upon thee. For, behold, the darkness shall cover the earth, and gross darkness the people: but the Lord shall arise upon thee, and his glory shall be seen upon thee. And the Gentiles shall come to thy light, and kings to the brightness of thy rising" (Isa. 60:1-3).

Wow! What a picture of success! The stage of life is set. The audience has gathered. The lights dim. The curtain of history rolls back, and there I am in center stage with the spotlight of destiny focused on me!

Now, I understand that this is a prophecy referring to the work of Christ, the Light of the world. But I believe that it has a secondary application to His followers, including women, who are also to be "the light of the world." (See Matt. 5:14.)

"For as the heavens are higher than the earth, so are my ways higher than your ways, and my thoughts than your thoughts. . . . For ye shall go out with joy, and be led forth with peace: the mountains and the hills shall break forth before you into singing, and all the trees of the field shall clap their hands'' (Isa. 55:9-12).

What a picture of success! All nature joins in applauding what God is able to do through His people. If I am God's woman, that is a picture of *my* success! I believe that God has a very special part for me to play, a part of the script that He has planned for me from the time I was nestled in the warmth of my mother's womb. Am I ready?

Am I ready to step out into the spotlight of destiny? Do I know my lines? What part is God expecting me to play in the drama that is about to unfold?

5. *I don't feel like a star.* "To tell you the truth, right now I don't feel like stepping into the spotlight," Carla confided. "My husband left me for another woman, and my kids are no longer in the church. I don't feel much like a success. Surely God doesn't want to use me!"

Oh, but He does! "High and low, rich and poor, all have a work to do for the Master. Everyone is called to action" (Ellen G. White, *Selected Messages,* book 1, p. 266).

The facts are that Carla is a woman of high worth. She is a woman of destiny, whether she feels like one or not. She is still a daughter of the King of kings. She is still special to Him. She still has a work to do for God, a work that no one else can do.

If she, in faith, talks and acts success, the feelings will come. That is one of the psychological rules of life. Positive feelings follow positive thoughts and positive actions.

Remember Gideon and his band of Israelites? They felt defeated, powerless, useless, against so many Midianites. But God said, "Blow your trumpets. Smash your pitchers. Act like success is yours, and it will be."

Remember Joshua and the children of Israel as they faced Jericho? They were ready to slink off and nurse their poor self-images. But God said, "Go out there and face the enemy.

March with your heads held high. Blow the trumpets.''
Success came following the actions of faith.

We Can Be Winners!

Twelve-year-old Wilma Rudolph decided to conquer all phases of women's sports. She went to her gym teacher one day and said, "If you will give me 10 minutes of your time, I will give you in return a world-class athlete."

The coach laughed at her audacity. She? A girl who sat out all the games on the bench? She who had been born prematurely, and then suffered two bouts with pneumonia and one with scarlet fever before coming down with polio that left a leg crooked and a foot twisted inward? She who had worn braces for six years before teaching herself to walk?

Wilma turned away, tears stinging her eyes.

"Wait," the coach called after her. "I'll give you the 10 minutes, but that's all I'll give you. Remember, I'll be busy with real world-class athletes, people who will be getting scholarships and winning gold medals."

Wilma was overjoyed. Every day she practiced for hours what she learned in each 10-minute session. By the age of 14 Wilma was a member of the University of Tennessee women's track team. At 16 she began training for the Olympics. At 20 she breezed to victories in the 100-meter and 200-meter dashes and helped the United States women's team reach first place in the 400-meter relay.

Then came the day when she walked out onto the stadium field in Rome. Nearly 80,000 fans began cheering wildly, "Vilma! Vilma! Vilma!"

Three times she stood atop the podium to receive a gold medal. Wilma Rudolph was the first woman in history to win three gold medals in track and field. Success for Wilma Rudolph meant conquering incredible odds, doing her best, winning the gold medal. Through years of practice she became a woman of excellence!

All of us Adventist women can be winners, no matter

where we were born or how much education we have. We can be women of excellence regardless of the mistakes we have made in the past or what problems we may face in the future. Despite suffering, abuse, setbacks, and handicaps we too can achieve. It doesn't matter what committees vote, or what others think. We can receive a gold medal in living.

Each of us can have success beyond our greatest dreams, for God created us to be women of excellence. He made us to be winners! He is on our cheering team!

Rate Yourself

On a score of 1 to 5, rate yourself on the following characteristics of a woman of excellence. Five is the best.

1. Walks with her head up, giving a smile to each person she meets.

      1   2   3   4   5

2. Looks people in the eye when she speaks.

      1   2   3   4   5

3. Volunteers her name first in a new association.

      1   2   3   4   5

4. Receives a compliment graciously, always saying "Thank you" but never playing down or playing up the value bestowed.

      1   2   3   4   5

5. Does not make excuses. Doesn't put herself down, but talks affirmatively about the progress she is making.

      1   2   3   4   5

6. Dresses and looks her best at all times.

      1   2   3   4   5

7. Walks erectly and briskly but with relaxed yet rapid pace in public.

1   2   3   4   5

8. Sits up front in meetings so she can exchange questions and comments with the speaker.

1   2   3   4   5

9. Gives her own name first when initiating or accepting a telephone call.

1   2   3   4   5

10. Seeks out women of excellence as friends and role models.

1   2   3   4   5

Personal Growth Exercises

1. Take a blank sheet of paper. Let it represent your total capacity or ability to achieve. Consider yourself. At what percent of your capacity are you working at the present time? Color that portion of the paper.

(Psychologist and philosopher William James estimated that the average person operated at about 10 percent of capacity. Even more recently anthropologist Margaret Mead estimated it to be 6 percent. More recently Herbert Otto has set it at 4 percent.)

2. Begin to appreciate the way God has made you. Fill in the following inventory.

A. Three leisure-time activities I enjoy:

_____   _____   _____

B. Three things I do well.

_____   _____   _____

C. Three achievements in my life:

_____   _____   _____

D. Three positive adjectives that describe me:

_____   _____   _____

E. Three things I like about my body, the way I look:

_____ _____ _____

3. Go back over your inventory in number 2 above. Use it as an outline for a prayer in which you thank God for each item on your list and the unique person He has made you to be.

4. Divide a sheet of paper into two columns. In the first column write the names of women in the Bible who project an image of success and high self-worth. Think of women who showed self-confidence and courage to become all that God had gifted them to become. In the second column, beside each name, write a brief description of her actions that show she was a woman of excellence.

Success Principle

Success is stretching toward my full potential through Christ, who enables me.

For Additional Reading

Heald, Cynthia. *Becoming a Woman of Excellence*, Nav-Press.

———. *Becoming a Woman of Freedom*, NavPress.

Kent, Carol. *Secret Longings of the Heart*, NavPress. (Previously titled *Secret Passions of the Christian Woman*.)

Painter, Alice. *The Challenge of Being a Woman*.

CHAPTER TWO

A Fulfilled Woman

IMPORTANT weekend guests were coming, and I wanted to make an impression. I determined to do it right, to meet everyone's expectations of how the wife of a conference president should entertain.

On Wednesday I finalized the menus and prepared a shopping list. On Thursday I cleaned the house from top to bottom, then shopped for groceries. On Friday I had nothing to do but cook and teach one class at the church school. I looked over my menu to see what I could do before leaving for school. The eggs! That would be easy.

I put the eggs in a pot with water, planning to bring them to a boil, cook them for one minute, take them off the burner, and let them sit while I went to school.

I waited until the water started to boil and then went to load the car with materials for class. I didn't want to waste even one minute! Everything was going like clockwork. I felt proud of my organization.

An hour later I opened the door to a house filled with smoke and an ominous popping sound. *Oh, no!* I thought. *The house is on fire and the light bulbs are popping!* Then I remembered the eggs!

I ran to the kitchen, grabbed the blackened pot from the burner, and hurried to fling open doors and windows. What a mess! Bits of egg and shell covered the floor, the cupboards, the ceiling, the window, the countertops, and the dining room table. There were even bits on the sofa!

I spent the next two hours scrubbing down the kitchen only to discover that Matt, our golden retriever puppy, had found a roll of toilet paper. Chewed-up bits of tissue were scattered in every room. The whole house had to be revacuumed.

There was no time for the fancy dishes I had planned! We dined rather simply that night on fruit salad and hastily purchased bagels and cream cheese!

And the smell! It was days before it went away! I impressed my guests, all right, but not the way I had hoped!

We can get ourselves into some embarrassing situations trying to live up to other people's expectations of us.

What Is My Role?

What is my role as an Adventist woman? To find out, I have often looked at other people's expectations: parents, grandparents, husband, children, church members, friends, neighbors, colleagues, and the community culture.

1. Parents and grandparents. In my mother I saw the role of a woman active in her community, visiting the sick, giving Bible studies, and leading out in the Women's Christian Temperance Union, garden clubs, and mothers' clubs.

From my Grandmother Eaton I got another view of what I should be: someone who stayed at home, made quilts, cooked nutritious meals, kept a clean house, and waited on her husband.

One day I heard Grandma talking to someone in her room. I tiptoed to the door and listened. She was praying. "Dear Lord, I feel so sorry for Oliver [her son, my father]. Estel is always on the go visiting or attending meetings. Help her stay home where she belongs!''

Which role should *I* fill? That of a community leader or a homemaker? Like many women, I've tried to fill both roles.

2. Husband. Soon after our wedding I asked Ron, ''What do you expect of me as your wife?''

''Just be yourself, Dorothy,'' he said with a smile. ''I love you just as you are. I have no expectations.''

But I soon discovered that he had plenty of expectations. He expected me to go visiting with him, lead out in children's ministries, pray in public, entertain people with little warning, and keep a clean house.

I became frustrated trying to fulfill the many expectations of parents, grandparents, and husband.

3. Church members. As if I weren't confused enough, I started trying to live up to the expectations of the church members. We arrived in our first district, Prince Albert, Saskatchewan, on a Thursday evening. On Saturday night there was a nominating committee meeting.

Ron came home to announce, ''Dorothy, they want you to be the church pianist.''

''You know I don't play the piano,'' I said.

''I told them that,'' Ron sighed, ''but they insisted. They said the pastor's wife had always been the pianist. There's no one else. If you don't do it, we'll just have to do without. So I said you'd do it.''

''But honey, I know only two or three hymns. There's no way I can do it,'' I gasped.

''I'll give you the hymns on Sunday, and you can practice all week. I'm sure you can manage.''

I managed, all right, sometimes with only one finger picking out the melody. In spite of lessons and hours of weekly practice, wonderful things do not happen when I sit down at the piano! Oh, the relief I felt when we were transferred to Saskatoon, where there were accomplished musicians and no one expected me to play.

4. Children. I have learned that there is no way I can be all that my children want me to be. I have a hard time measuring up to my children's expectations, even after the children are married and on their own. I found this out when I announced that their dad and I would spend Christmas in Mexico.

"But we expected that we'd all get together as a family for Christmas," our grown children wailed.

When we insisted that we needed a quiet vacation in the sun away from phones and all responsibilities, one of them remarked: "Mom and Dad must be getting senile!"

5. Culture. What people expect of a woman in a small town in southern Ohio is quite different from what is expected in metropolitan Los Angeles. What is quite acceptable in Saskatoon, Saskatchewan, is not at all the right thing to do in Bangalore, India.

According to the Protestant work ethic, with which Ron and I were raised, children must learn to work. Not so in caste-conscious India, where we served 16 years as missionaries. We insisted that our children make their own beds, iron their own clothes, and keep their rooms clean. A neighbor shook his head and said, "I wouldn't *want* my children to do what you *make* yours do."

6. God. It is bad enough trying to live up to the expectations of family, friends, and culture, but what about the expectations of God? What roles does He expect me to fill?

I think I have found the answer: the G Factor. We find the G Factor in the story of the lame man in Acts 3. Let's give him a name, Jonathan, and imagine what it might have been like for him that day so long ago.

The Feast Day

On this particular morning Jonathan sat near the gate called Beautiful. It was almost time for the meeting to begin. Eagerly he watched the approaching worshipers.

Ah! There come two now. They look like important

people. They carry themselves erect, walking with assurance.

Lifting bony arms, Jonathan cried in a quivering voice, "Alms! Alms for the poor cripple!"

The two strangers stopped and looked at the beggar sitting on his dirty mat, his withered legs folded in front of him. The older of the two stooped and took Jonathan's two hands in his own, saying, "I know you want money, but I don't have any. However, I have something that is better than money. In the name of Jesus Christ of Nazareth, rise up and walk."

As he spoke, the stranger straightened up, still gripping Jonathan's frail hands in his own strong fisherman hands. Jonathan felt a rippling, tingling sensation move through his arms, down the trunk of his body, into his legs. He felt his legs straighten, the bones and muscles growing and taking the shape of those belonging to a healthy man. The stranger let go and Jonathan stood alone.

"Praise the Lord!" he shouted. "I can stand!" He took a cautious step forward. "I can walk!" The Bible says that he went with Peter and John into the Temple, leaping, shouting, and praising God. And because of Jonathan's witness, a multitude believed and were baptized.

We find the G Factor in Acts 3:6: "Silver and gold have I none; but such as I have give I thee."

Peter and John gave the beggar a gift, but it was not what he expected. They couldn't give money because they had none to give. They were broke. Instead, they gave what they possessed, the power of God to heal withered legs.

The Gift Factor

That is the G Factor—the Gift Factor. We cannot give what we do not possess. God does not expect us to give to others what He has not first given to us. As Adventist women we are to share with people, not according to their expectations, but according to how the Lord has gifted us.

I was slow to learn the lesson of the G Factor. When we arrived in Bangalore, India, I was asked to lead the choir.

Although I turned down the honor of directing, they persuaded me to join.

The first practice was disastrous. I was hitting an unhappy medium somewhere between the alto and the soprano parts when the choir director threw up his hands. The music stopped. Very kindly he said, looking in my direction, "Those who cannot carry the tune should not be in the choir."

I did not show up for the next rehearsal, much to everyone's relief! Music is not a gift that I have to give. Any attempt to give what I don't have brings frustration.

Teaching and writing are gifts that I *do* have. When I try giving what I have, then I really enjoy the experience.

Giving What I Have

Operating by the G Factor has made a difference in my life. I no longer am plagued by other people's expectations of me. The important thing is not what others think, but what God thinks. I know that He does not expect me to give to others what He has not already given to me.

The gift of singing and playing the piano I may not have, but such as I have—a listening ear—*that* I give unto you. I cannot produce a financial statement, but such as I have—the gift of drama, fun, and laughter—*that* I give unto you.

Esther's Gifts

Once there was a woman so lovely that she won a beauty contest and ended up in the king's harem. But Esther had more than beauty. She had a strong character, a love for the Lord and for her people. When she discovered Haman's plot to exterminate the Jews, she was ready to place all her gifts on the line. She understood that her gifts had brought her to the kingdom for such a time as that.

Could it be that I, an Adventist woman, have also come to the kingdom for this hour in earth's history? What gifts, dreams, friendships, and interests do I have? What will not get done in my corner of the world if I do not do it?

Why has God gifted me? What does He want me to do with my gifts for the building up of His kingdom?

Esther used all the gifts in her possession: beauty, hospitality, and an understanding of what makes people tick. She made herself as attractive as she could, and then she went in before the king and invited him and his chief adviser to a banquet. Eventually she revealed her identity and Haman's intrigue. In sharing her gifts, she risked all her security and future.

I may not win the Miss Universe Contest, but I have other gifts. I have abilities and dreams. I have talents and opportunities. What am I doing with what I have?

Rate Yourself

Below are a few of the gifts Adventist women possess. Check those that you have and are thus able to share.

__shopping	__saving money	__garage sales
__speaking	__relating to kids	__sewing
__singing	__storytelling	__crafts
__cooking	__playing instrument	__having fun
__organization	__cleaning	__parties
__writing	__baking	__gardening
__decorating	__flower arranging	__encouragement
__nature study	__thoughtfulness	__listening
__helping	__selling	__visiting
__sensitivity	__common sense	__driving
__fixing things	__conflict management	__teaching
__drawing	__Bible study	__prayer

Personal Growth Exercises

1. Can you think of a time you got into hot water trying to live up to other people's expectations? Can you relate your own version of a "kitchen catastrophe"?

2. Take a sheet of typing paper. Fold it in half one way and into half the other way. Fold it once more into half. Open

it up and you will have eight sections. At the top of each section write one of the following labels: parents, friends, husband, children, neighbors, church members, colleagues, and TV culture. Under each one write its expectations for you.

3. Make a list of all the church offices you have held. Which ones were enjoyable experiences? Which were frustrating efforts? In which were you trying to give what you did not possess?

4. Read the parable of the talents in Matthew 25:14-30. Then make a list of your talents, gifts, and abilities. Try to think of at least 10 items.

5. Read the chapter titled "Talents" in *Christ's Object Lessons*, by Ellen G. White. What other talents does she suggest that you had not listed? Add them to your list now. What does she suggest you can do to increase your number of talents?

6. Choose one talent that you would like to see improved. What can you do to enlarge that talent? Are there classes you can attend, a correspondence course you can take, books you can read, or someone you know who can help you toward growth in that area? Make a definite plan to strengthen and use that one talent. Take the first step this week.

7. Read 1 Corinthians 12, Romans 12, and Ephesians 4. Make a list of the gifts of the Spirit. Circle those that you think you have. Is there any relationship between the gifts?

8. If you have never taken a "Spiritual Gifts Inventory," ask your pastor to give you one. Better yet, attend a Spiritual Gifts Seminar.

Success Principle

God does not expect us to give to others what He has not first given to us.

For Additional Reading

Blanchard, Tim. *A Practical Guide to Finding and Using Your Spiritual Gifts*. Tyndale House.

Crabb, Rachel with Hart, Raeann. *The Personal Touch:*

Encouraging Others Through Hospitality. NavPress.

Mitchell, Marcia L. *Giftedness: Discovering Your Areas of Strength.* Bethany House.

Painter, Alice. *God's Gifted People: Discovering Your Personality as a Gift.* Augsburg. (Includes Myers-Briggs Personality Test.)

CHAPTER THREE

A Spiritual Woman

*I*T WAS a gray, cloudy Sunday in Belfast, Ireland. The Carmichael family were returning from church when they met an old woman carrying a heavy bundle.

"Look at that poor woman!" Amy said. "She needs help!" Running to her side, she offered, "Here, let me help you."

Instantly two of her brothers were at her side, lifting down the heavy package from the woman's back. One brother shouldered the bundle while Amy and the other brother took hold of the woman's feeble arms and steadied her as she walked. Respectable church folks frowned as they saw the Carmichaels assisting the disheveled old woman.

"It was a horrid moment," Amy admitted afterward. "We were only two boys and a girl, and not at all exalted Christians. We hated doing it. Crimson all over (at least we felt crimson, soul and body of us), we plodded on, a wet wind blowing us about, and blowing, too, the rags of that poor old woman, till she seemed like a bundle of feathers, and we unhappily mixed up with them."

At that moment of embarrassment they came to a fountain

beside the road, bubbling upward in the gray drizzle, and a verse of Scripture Amy had memorized flashed into her mind.

"Gold, silver, precious stones, wood, hay, stubble; every man's work shall be made manifest: for the day shall declare it, because it shall be revealed by fire; and the fire shall try every man's work of what sort it is. If any man's work abide . . ."

So clearly came the words of 1 Corinthians 3:12-14 that Amy turned to see who had spoken. She saw nothing but the muddy street, people walking home from church, and the fountain bubbling in the mist.

"I said nothing to anyone," Amy later wrote, "but I knew that something had happened that had changed life's values. Nothing could ever matter again but the things that were eternal."

Not long after that she felt that God was calling her to be a missionary. She spent the rest of her life, more than 50 years, as a single missionary first in Japan and later in south India.

In Amy's life I see nine characteristics of a godly woman. We can outline them using the letters of the word "s-p-i-r-i-t-u-a-l" as an acrostic.

S—Sense of the eternal. A spiritual woman will have her priorities in order, understanding that only what she has done for Christ will last.

While attending a religious convention in Glasgow, Amy Carmichael joined a friend for lunch at a restaurant where the food was poorly cooked. Someone complained. Amy thought, *What difference does that make in the light of eternity?*

Not long after that, Amy's mother took her shopping in Belfast for a new evening dress. The shopkeeper brought out his loveliest silks and satins. As Amy looked at the beautiful cloth, she remembered thinking, *What are parties and fine clothes in light of eternity?*

"Mother, I can't do this," Amy whispered. "I don't want a new evening dress. Other things are now more important to me."

Embarrassed, her mother mumbled an apology to the shopkeeper, and they walked out.

In the light of eternity I wonder how important are some of the things on which I spend my time and money?

Lord, give me a sense of the eternal. Help me get my priorities straight.

P—Prayer is important. Prayer is vital to the life of a spiritual woman. To her, God is real—someone interested in all the circumstances of her life.

Becky Tirabassi, author of *Releasing God's Power,* had very little time for God before attending a prayer seminar. One of the speakers said, "Prayerlessness is a sin."

Becky was shocked. As the truth of the statement dawned on her she thought, *I make time for what I consider a priority. Where in all my activity is a time for God? Yet I say I love Him.*

Before the seminar was over, Becky had decided to pray one hour every day. She has developed an eight-point plan that easily takes her through an hour of prayer, Bible study, and meditation every morning.

Ellen G. White observes, "It would be well for us to spend a thoughtful hour each day in contemplation of the life of Christ" (*The Desire of Ages*, p. 83).

In commenting in her diary about an hour she had spent in prayer, Amy Carmichael wrote: "The hour passed like five minutes."

What in my life can be condensed or discarded so that I can spend an hour with my Lord each day?

Lord, forgive me for the sin of prayerlessness. Help me find time to spend with You.

I—Immersed in the Word. To the spiritual woman Bible study is not a tiresome chore, but one that she looks forward to with anticipation. She thinks, *What message will God have for me today?*

Becky Tirabassi keeps a notebook in which she records messages she gets from God through sermons as well as

31

through her reading. Every day she reads at least one chapter from the New Testament, one from the Old Testament, and one from Proverbs.

Ione Richardson, author of *Bouquets, With Love From Jesus*, likes to make a verse of Scripture her own by paraphrasing it. She writes down a plan of action based on that verse and a prayer of response to the message she has received.

Susanna Wesley, mother of 19 children, still found time to spend two hours every day in Bible study. She had a set time when she put aside household chores and went to her room to study.

Ruth Bell Graham, wife of Evangelist Billy Graham, leaves an open Bible on the coffee table. That way, whenever she has a few moments, she can read a verse or two and relax. She also memorizes verses, repeating them as she drives, irons, or does other household tasks.

Thank You, Lord, for Your Word. Help me plan a time every day when I can immerse myself in it.

R—Recognizes the importance of silence. Godly women obey the command ''Be still, and know that I am God.'' They take time not only to study and pray but also to listen to God's voice.

Amy Carmichael had the habit of spending long periods in quietness after Bible study and prayer. Out of these periods of meditation came many of her poems and songs. Once when struggling with the thought of being single, she tells of going away alone to a cave in a mountain to pray and listen for the ''still small voice.'' In the solitude of her retreat God assured her, ''None of them that trust in Me shall be desolate.'' From there she went on to start Dohnavur Fellowship, which rescued many temple prostitutes.

Lord, I want to be a woman who takes time to listen to Your voice. Help me learn how to enjoy solitude in the midst of my busy schedule.

I—Invites Jesus to walk with her in all the circumstances

of her life. The Lord walks with her through the tough times of life as well as the easy times.

Ruth Graham has, though married, lived much of her life as a single mother of five. How has she survived? God has shared the tough times with her.

She admits to crying over her Bible as she has sought to ease her loneliness and find answers to deal with the disappointment of having two sons turn away from the Lord.

Ruth tells about one time when she stayed up all night out of concern for her son Ned. As she fellowshipped with the Lord, He led her to Philippians 4:6: "Have no anxiety about anything, but in everything by prayer and supplication with thanksgiving let your requests be made known to God" (RSV).

She says, "Suddenly I realized the missing ingredient to my prayers had been thanksgiving. So I sat there and thanked God for all that Ned was and all he had meant to me through the years. . . . When we are most concerned, we should start thanking the Lord for the lessons He is teaching us through the tough times. And invariably it is through those tough times that the Scriptures really come to life" (Dale Hanson Burke, "Ruth Bell Graham: Tough and Tender Moments," *Today's Christian Woman*, Nov./Dec. 1991, p. 53).

T—Talks easily about the Lord and His goodness. The spiritual woman is not embarrassed to give a testimony in church or to ask God's blessing on her food in a restaurant. It is as natural for her to talk about Jesus as it is to talk about her children or a close friend.

As Ellen White puts it: "If we are Christ's, our sweetest thoughts will be of Him. We shall love to talk of Him; and as we speak to one another of His love, our hearts will be softened by divine influences" (*The Desire of Ages,* p. 83).

Anne Hutchinson was a woman always ready to talk about the Lord. Women from Boston flocked to her home to hear her explain the Scriptures and share her experience with God. Sometimes as many as 80 women crowded into her house to learn about God's grace and power. In the end she was banished from the colony for talking about the Lord.

If I were put on trial for speaking of the goodness of the Lord, I hope there would be enough evidence to convict me!

Lord, help me be more like Anne Hutchinson, so excited about the reality of my experience with You that I must talk about it.

U—Understand God's call. Great women of faith have always understood God's call to service. They have sensed their place in the scheme of things, their part in God's plan to save the human race.

Amy Carmichael tells about counseling with a friend and then going to her room to ask the Lord what He wanted her to do. She wrote to her mother, "As clearly as I ever heard you speak, I heard Him say 'Go ye.' I never heard it just so plainly before; I cannot be mistaken, for I know He spoke. He says 'Go,' and I cannot stay."

Ruth Bell Graham was not called to be a cross-cultural missionary in some far off corner of the globe, but to be a support to her famous evangelist husband. About this she says: "All my life, I had felt called for mission work there in China, and I only came to college to prepare myself for that work. But I think the Lord must have given me that intense longing for a purpose, so that I could have the understanding and the sense of fulfillment that I now receive from Bill's work" (James Schaffer and Colleen Todd, *Christian Wives*, p. 63).

Lord, help me understand when You call me for a specific part of Your plan, and make me willing to follow Your directions for my life.

A—Awareness of God's presence. The spiritual woman has a keen sense of God's presence in her life. She is aware of what He is doing in the lives of her family, her church, and the political structures of the world. Through all the play and interplay of human events she can see God's hand at work.

Ruth Graham could have become discouraged when two of her sons turned their backs on God for a time, but she held firmly to her faith in God, recognizing that He was working in their lives. She says, "Our children never outreach God's reach. . . . Sometimes we forget God is omnipotent, omnipresent, omniscient, and eternal. Our children can run—but God knows where they are, and God is watching over them" (Dale Hanson Burke, *ibid*.).

In a time of particular darkness after the death of a dear friend, Amy Carmichael wrote, "We have seen our God's forethinking care for us proved in very many ways since that day of sudden desolation." Amy was aware that no matter what the difficulty, God is still in control.

Lord, open my eyes that I might see Your hand at work in my life today. Help me never forget that You are in control, regardless of how things look.

L—Loves people. A woman who is close to God inevitably finds herself loving all for whom He died, even the most unlovely.

Amy Carmichael loved the prostitutes, and Mother Teresa loves the castoffs of society: the destitute, dying, abandoned, and forsaken. Mary Jo Copeland looked with compassion on the homeless of Minneapolis and started Sharing and Caring Hands.

Chessie Harris loved neglected children in America's South and wanted to save them from pain, poverty, and despair. She began taking in foster children. Before she retired, Chessie had mothered more than 800 children!

Lord, help me be a woman stirred with compassion for the needs of people, willing to reach out to others with Your love.

Rate Yourself

On a scale of 1 to 5, how would you rate yourself in the following areas of spirituality? Five is the best.

1. My priorities reflect my sense of eternal values.

    1   2   3   4   5

2. Prayer is a vital part of my life.

    1   2   3   4   5

3. I daily immerse myself in the Word of God.

    1   2   3   4   5

4. I have discovered the transforming power of silence.

    1   2   3   4   5

5. I invite Jesus to walk with me through all the circumstances of my life, the tough times as well as the good times.

    1   2   3   4   5

6. I find it easy to talk about God's goodness to me.

    1   2   3   4   5

7. I understand the particular plan God has for my life.

    1   2   3   4   5

8. I am aware of God's presence at work in my world.

    1   2   3   4   5

9. I love people of all situations and cultures.

    1   2   3   4   5

Personal Growth Exercises

1. Give yourself the gift of solitude. Go away for several hours. Take no radio or cassette player. Read, meditate on Scripture, contemplate God's handiwork in nature, and be totally silent.

2. Plan a program for a "thoughtful hour each day in contemplation of the life of Christ" (*The Desire of Ages*, p. 83). Read one chapter of *The Desire of Ages* each day along with the scriptural passages on which it is based. Keep a

notebook of your discoveries. Write out quotations that appeal to you. The 87 chapters will take you through three months of personal devotions.

3. For one month keep a diary of things that show God's hand at work in your life. At the end of each day write down all the evidences you have seen of His protectin̄g Document answers to prayer. Write down news items a fulfillment of prophecy.

4. On Friday evening write out a brief testimo God has blessed you during the week. What do you especially grateful for during the past seven da opportunity presents itself, share that testimony o̱r

5. Choose a verse of Scripture that means a to you. Insert your name where appropriate. Rewrite it, showing what it means to you in your current circumstances. What message is God trying to give you?

Success Principle

"Seek ye first the kingdom of God" (Matt. 6:33). "Give him first place in your life" (TLB).

For Additional Reading

Christenson, Evelyn. *What Happens When Women Pray.* Victor.

————. *What Happens When We Pray for Our Families.* Victor.

Kidd, Sue Monk. *When the Heart Waits: Spiritual Direction for Life's Sacred Questions.* Harper and Row.

Klug, Ronald. *How to Keep a Spiritual Journal.* Thomas Nelson.

Roberts, Lee. *Praying God's Will for My Husband.* Thomas Nelson.

Senter, Ruth. *Longing for Love: Conversations With a Compassionate Heavenly Father*. NavPress.

Tirabassi, Becky. *Let Prayer Change Your Life: How You Can Release God's Power*. Thomas Nelson.

Urquhart, Colin. *My Dear Child: Listening to God's* ██████ Creation House.

██████, Kathleen. *Amy Carmichael*. Bethany House Pub-

CHAPTER FOUR

A Focused Woman

*T*HE shrill blast of a whistle sounds. The race is about to begin, and you are one of the contestants.

"On your mark!"

You place your right foot just behind the white line. You bend your knees and lean forward.

"Get ready!"

You take a deep breath to calm your racing heart.

"Get set!"

You look up, ready to fix your eyes on the goal, but wait a minute! Where is the finish line? "How far do we have to run?" you ask.

"There is no finish line. Just run as fast as you can. On your mark! Ready! Set! Go!"

Who of us would run under those conditions? Who wants to run in a race without a finish line? How can we be winners if there is no goal? Just so, if we would be winners in the game called life, we *must* have a goal. We've got to know where we're going, or how will we ever get there?

Alice in Wonderland

All too often I have felt like Alice in Wonderland when she came to the crossroads.

"Cheshire-puss," she says to the cat, "would you tell me, please, which way I ought to go from here?"

"That depends a good deal on where you want to get to," replied the cat.

"I don't much care where I go," said Alice.

"Then it doesn't matter which road you take," said the cat.

Did you know that 97 percent of women go through life much like Alice in Wonderland? Researchers tell us that only 3 percent of us have definite, specific goals that are written on paper, goals that can be seen and measured. Three percent of us know where we are going and will likely succeed in getting there.

The rest of us can learn something from the caterpillars in Jean Henri Fabre's experiment. Fabre arranged the caterpillars around the rim of a flowerpot so that the lead caterpillar actually touched the last caterpillar, thus making a complete circle. In the center of the pot he put the food enjoyed by that particular species of caterpillar.

The caterpillars started walking around that flowerpot. Around and around and around they went. For seven full days and seven full nights they marched in a circle, until they finally dropped dead from starvation.

The caterpillars' mistake is one Adventist women often make. We confuse activity with accomplishment. We are all busy. The question is What are we accomplishing? Without definite, visible, written goals we can easily get involved in circular activity that achieves nothing of lasting value. Activity does not lead to accomplishment until it is focused on a specific goal.

The Line of Separation

What is it that separates women of excellence from women of mediocrity?

It is not time. Dr. Ida Scudder, founder of Vellore Christian Medical School, lived with the same time constraints as we. It is not family responsibilities. Ellen White, who has more than 50 books to her credit, faced the problems of juggling career and family needs in days that were no longer than ours.

It is not our race. Marian Anderson struggled against racial prejudice and became a woman of excellence. It is not beauty. Eleanor Roosevelt admitted to feeling like an ugly duckling, but she accomplished much. It is not a handicap. Joni Eareckson Tada writes books and paints pictures despite the fact that she is a quadriplegic.

What makes the difference? A cause. A destination. A goal. A purpose. When we know where we are going, it is possible to find a way to get there regardless of the obstacles in our path.

"Grandma, do you know Daniel?" our 5-year-old grandson, Calvin, asked one day.

"Yes," I replied. "Why do you ask?"

"Grandma, did you know that Daniel did it on purpose?" he continued.

His mother and I laughed at Calvin's version of Daniel 1:8, but the truth is that Calvin had it right. Daniel did what he did because that was his goal. He did do it on purpose! Without such a purpose he would not likely have maintained his faith through the difficulties he faced.

A Woman With a Purpose

Estel Halterman Eaton was a woman with a purpose. At the age of 62 she decided to realize the dream of her life, to become a nurse. She went back to school and graduated with the highest marks in her class. She lived another 25 years, working, earning, learning, and traveling.

It is never too late to have a purpose, to set some goals. It is never too late to become a woman of excellence, to realize the dream of a lifetime.

When I was 15 I remember writing down four specific goals: become a teacher, marry a minister, go overseas as a missionary, and write a book by the time I am 35. I did become a teacher. I married a minister. We went as missionaries to India. And I now have had 10 books published. However, I was eight years off on my timing.

What are my goals? What do I want to accomplish during the next year? The next five years? The next 10 years? During my lifetime? Have I put those goals on paper?

The Power of Written Goals

I'll never forget the first time I visited Niagara Falls and heard the roar of the water and felt its mist on my face. The water rushed on, a never-ending cascade of power. I thought of the billions of gallons of water that must have gone over those falls in the centuries since the Flood, only to dissipate into nothingness.

Then one day a man with a goal harnessed that power. He directed some of that falling water toward a specific target and created billions of kilowatt hours of electricity to turn the wheels of industry and light thousands of homes.

What a difference it makes when activity is directed toward a specific target! Putting my goals on paper is like building a generator at Niagara Falls. A mysterious something happens when I write down definite goals. Power is released, and things start to happen.

Women With Goals

"What is worse than being born blind?" someone once asked Helen Keller.

She quickly replied, "To have sight and no vision."

Helen Keller had no sight, but oh, did she have a vision! She set her goal to graduate from college, and she did! She set a goal to awaken people everywhere to the possibilities of the blind, and she became known around the world.

Florence Nightingale was able to do much for the cause of

nursing because she had a vision of what the nursing profession could become.

Joan of Arc's name is remembered more than 500 years after her death because she had a definite goal of what she needed to do for France.

Mother Teresa would not have received the Nobel Peace Prize had she not been given a mission, a purpose in life, to help the poorest of the poor on the streets of Calcutta.

Golda Meir, Margaret Thatcher, Corazon Aquino, and Indira Gandhi all became leaders of their countries because of specific goals they set for themselves.

Elizabeth Blackwell became the first woman in the United States to graduate from medical school because she had a dream of what she wanted to be.

The Stages of Accomplishing a Goal

In his book *Be All You Can Be*, John Maxwell gives the six stages of accomplishing a goal: I thought it. I caught it. I bought it. I sought it. I got it. I taught it. I can see how I followed those six stages in writing my first devotional book, *This Is the Day*.

I thought it. I first had the thought when I was about 15. Because a teacher encouraged me, I got the idea it might be possible. That is something I wanted to do someday.

I caught it. At a Pathfinder Camporee near Bangalore, India, I taught the Sabbath school lesson. Afterward a youth leader from the General Conference approached me. "Have you ever thought of writing a book?" he asked. "You communicate well with this age level. I would like to see you write a junior devotional." I agreed to try. I wrote down my goal: to write a junior devotional.

I bought it. I went home and invested in my dream. I set up files for each month. I began collecting stories that actually happened on each day of the year. I devoted many hours to research, writing, and rewriting. I asked God to help me.

I sought it. I sent off a one-month sample to the committee in charge of daily devotionals. They approved my plan, and I could now believe that it would really happen. I continued research and writing for eight years until finally it was complete. I could imagine the book in print. I worked to make it a reality.

I got it. The day finally came when I received a copy of the completed book in the mail. The book was published. It was sold in all the Adventist Book Centers. I could hold my dream in my hand. I had accomplished what I had set out to achieve.

I taught it. As a result of my success I was asked to speak to school groups and writers' clubs. I shared the steps I had followed to get a book published. I shared secrets of writing something that would sell. At every opportunity I passed on what I had learned.

Mary Had a Dream

I admire Mary Jane McLeod because of the way she set goals and then found a way to make those dreams a reality in spite of obstacles of poverty and prejudice.

Mary Jane McLeod was born into a Black family in South Carolina 12 years after Abraham Lincoln had freed the slaves. Although theoretically Mary was as free as any White girl, she soon learned there were some things White girls did that she couldn't do. The thing that bothered her most was that she couldn't read.

One Saturday afternoon when Mary was 10 years old she went with her mother to the home of some White neighbors. The two girls invited Mary Jane into their playhouse. She pretended that she was the nursemaid and rocked a beautiful doll while her hostesses pretended to be Southern belles. While Mary rocked the doll, she noticed a book lying on a table. She reached over and picked it up.

"Put that down!" screamed one of the girls.

"I won't hurt it," said Mary Jane. "I just want to feel it."

"No!" shouted the other sister. "Books are for people who can't read. You can't read."

Mary put the book down and placed the doll on the chair. Then she ran out of the playhouse and down the pathway, where she met her mother and sobbed out the story.

"I *will* learn to read," Mary Jane said.

Her mother smiled and said nothing, for she knew that her daughter could not go to school. She had to work in the cotton fields.

Mary Jane picked cotton, but as she did she chanted a little prayer, "I want to read! I want to read! Please, dear God, let me go to school."

Before long a teacher came to the area and started a school. Mary Jane attended. Later she went away to college and became a teacher. She eventually opened her own school in Daytona, Florida. This school grew so large that it became a college, and Mary Jane McLeod Bethune was its first president.

As a result of her position, Mary Jane met many important people, and wherever she went she shared how God had answered her prayers and helped her realize the goal she had set for herself that day when she held a book in her hands for the first time.

Mary Jane McLeod Bethune had a dream. She thought it, caught it, bought it, and sought it. Eventually, with God's help, she got it and taught it.

Rate Yourself

What are some of the hindrances you have faced in reaching the goals of your life? What has kept you from being all you could be? Please check those that apply to your situation.

___Insufficient education   ___Physically unattractive

___Lack of money   ___Sex discrimination

___Uncooperative spouse   ___Racial discrimination

___Negative family upbringing   ___Got in with wrong crowd

__Chose wrong profession   __Family responsibilities

__Substance abuse   __Unsympathetic boss

__Limited family support   __Physical handicaps

__Shyness   __Lack of connections

__Bad luck   __Illness

Now go back and put a big, bold X through the whole list. Difficulties are no reason to cop out on your dreams. It isn't the circumstances of life that make us winners or losers; it is how we react to the circumstances. It is not what we have that determines our success; it is what we do with what we have.

Personal Growth Exercises

1. Copy the chart below:

My Goals for This Year

Area	Goal	Strategy
Physical		
Mental		
Social		
Spiritual		
Family		
Professional		
Church/Community		

Write down at least one goal for each area of your life.

Include other areas that fit your situation. Write down at least one concrete thing you can do to advance toward each goal. Fill in more strategies as you think of them.

2. Use a calendar to set your goals for the next month. What will you do? When will you do it? How will you achieve it?

3. Use a weekly calendar or a journal to set your activities for the week. Make sure that weekly goals help you reach monthly and yearly goals. Review the list daily.

4. Make a list of your daily priorities. What will you do today that will move you toward your goals? Put those things at the head of your "To Do List."

5. Assemble support material for each of your goals. Have a file for each goal. Into each put clippings, articles, books, tapes, estimates, brochures, samples, and other items that will help you reach your goal.

6. Reward yourself for accomplishing your goals. Ceremonialize each achievement.

7. Pray about your goals. Psalm 37:4 says: "He shall give thee the desires of thine heart."

Success Principle

Activity does not lead to accomplishment until it is focused on a specific goal.

For Additional Reading

Littauer, Florence. *It Takes so Little to Be Above Average*. Harvest House.

Maxwell, John. *Be All You Can Be*. Victor Books.

CHAPTER FIVE

A Supportive Woman

T was a grand occasion on Capitol Hill in Washington, D.C. Some of the most powerful leaders of the United States had gathered with their wives for a luncheon to honor an aging little woman in a white sari trimmed with blue.

As she entered the room, her bare feet in worn sandals, all talking stopped. The crowd stood to honor this tiny four-foot-eleven-inch woman. The great men suddenly felt all choked up. They had come to honor Mother Teresa, winner of the Nobel Peace Prize, but instead they felt that she was honoring them.

Her blue eyes sparkled amid the sea of wrinkles on her brown face as she talked of the need for love, mercy, and compassion in the world.

We can imagine her holding a dying man in her arms, someone her helpers have just brought in from the gutters of Calcutta. He smells of urine and excrement, but she holds him close. She talks to him softly as she tries to get him to drink a little broth.

We can picture her holding an infant girl with diarrhea,

whom her helpers have just discovered in a garbage bin. She calls the baby sweet love-names as she drops milk onto her tongue. No one is too sick, too demented, too smelly or dirty for Mother Teresa's love and attention.

We marvel at what one woman has been able to accomplish for humanity, but she has not established her homes of mercy throughout the world singlehandedly. Around her is a large personal network of people who have helped her achieve that distinction. There are the hundreds of nuns who roam the streets, looking for the sick, the dying, the orphan, and the leper. There are the generous people who donate land, money, food, and clothing. And there are the government officials who give her permission to operate her homes. Mother Teresa built her success by expanding her network.

We Can't Do It Alone

No woman is an island. We do not walk alone. None of us live to ourselves, accomplishing everything on our own. (See Rom. 14:7.) We cannot be a success in life alone. What we become depends a great deal on the people in our personal networks.

Sally Ride reached for the stars and succeeded. She realized her dream of becoming the first American woman in space, but she did not do it alone. Sally's personal network made her place in history possible: her family, her neighbors, the space-shuttle crew, officials at NASA, politicians, and even the president of the United States. Sally Ride built her success by expanding her network.

Margaret Thatcher successfully led her country as prime minister for more than a decade. She presided over the renaissance of prosperity in Great Britain, but she did not do it alone. Mrs. Thatcher's personal network made her achievements possible. Her network included presidents, prime ministers, kings, queens, members of Parliament, bankers, corporation executives, as well as family and friends. Margaret Thatcher built her success by expanding her network.

Mary Jo Copeland founded Sharing and Caring Hands, a day shelter for the poor in Minneapolis. In it she cares for more than 500 homeless individuals whom she feeds regularly. She welcomes each with the same warm smile she has for friends. She offers them soup, a hot shower, clean clothes, and a comfortable place to sleep. But Mary Jo Copeland doesn't do all this alone. In her network are ministers, merchants, bankers, and donors. There are dozens of volunteers who share the load. There are family members and friends who give her support. Mary Jo Copeland built her success by expanding her network.

What Is a Network?

Network is a modern word for a person's circle of contacts. This circle consists of six recognizable levels of association.

Level One: Very Close Friends. These are people we share with on an intimate level. With these special friends we can share the deeper things of our souls: our hopes, fears, joys, and concerns. These people at the core of our network are those with whom we feel absolutely comfortable. We may have only two or three people at this level.

Level Two: Good Friends. These are people we see often because we enjoy being with them. We eat, camp, party, talk, and travel together. We share, but not as intimately as with our very close friends. We generally can handle 12 to 20 on this level of friendship.

Level Three: Casual Friends. In this group we may have 50 to 100 people. Here is where neighbors and church family fit in. There are warm feelings when we meet, we share many of the same group experiences, but we do not share our lives with them in the same way as we do groups from levels one and two.

Level Four: Work Associates and Extended Family. We see these people on a daily basis in connection with work, or perhaps only occasionally at family gatherings. Here are our aunts, uncles, cousins, and colleagues.

Level Five: Faraway Friends. These are people who have moved from the inner circles of our network toward the outer edge. Either they moved or we moved. We exchange cards or yearly letters and look them up when we pass through their towns.

Level Six: Acquaintances. These are people we have met. We know their names and a little about them, but we don't really count them as our friends. The number in this group may be in the hundreds or thousands, depending on our opportunities for contacts.

Reasons for Expanding Our Networks

Did you know that as much as 85 percent of members baptized into the Seventh-day Adventist Church come from among the personal networks of the church members? When evangelists are successful in their public meetings, it is because they are working with a church that has members with large personal networks. This is one good reason to expand our networks.

Church growth specialists tell us that a new member needs at least seven close or good friends within the church if that member is to remain. Research shows that as the number of friends within the church goes down, the incidence of apostasy goes up. This is a second good reason to expand our networks to include new members.

Success in many areas of our lives can be enhanced by enlarging our personal networks. We cannot have accomplishments alone. We must depend on other people. Women especially need other women.

How to Expand Our Networks

The woman who wants to expand her personal network will cultivate six specific skills according to career coach Adele Scheele: experience doing, risk linking, show belonging, exhibit specializing, finding a mentor, and sharing what she knows.

1. Experience doing. The successful woman is continually seeking new experiences, learning new skills, and gaining new information. The woman expands her network as she attends classes, workshops, and seminars, participates in sports, volunteers for church work, and gets involved in community activities.

2. Risk linking. The woman of excellence will seek out ways to meet new people, especially those who are successful.

Tania Torres, a Brazilian task force worker in Alaska, wanted to expand her network so that she could witness for Jesus. She enrolled in an English conversation course. Before long her new friends invited her to birthday parties and weddings, where she met more people. She and her husband taught in a community summer recreation program, again so they could meet new people.

3. Show belonging. The successful woman doesn't sit on the sidelines, but gets involved. She participates in group sponsored activities and shows her enthusiasm. She is a booster for any group she joins, someone who helps build community spirit. By participating, cooperating, and expressing enthusiasm the successful woman shows belonging.

Dr. Ruth Lennox, of Abbotsford, British Columbia, shows her belonging to the community by participating in professional organizations and volunteering for a community clinic.

Beverly Moody is deeply involved in the social life of Aleknagik, Alaska. She attends community concerts and helps out with school functions.

4. Exhibit specializing. The woman of excellence will use her gifts to bless someone else. By finding a need and filling it, she draws people and success to her doorstep.

Jasmine Jacob was a teacher in Benton Harbor, Michigan, until she visited India and saw the condition of children in the villages. She saw a need for a sponsorship program to help children get an education so that they could rise above the circumstances of their lives. In the basement of her home, with a few supportive friends, she began REACH International, which today is caring for thousands of children in orphanages and schools in India, Romania, Rwanda, Burma, Bangladesh, Ethiopia, Philippines, Sri Lanka, Thailand, Zaire, and Zimbabwe. By finding a need and filling it, Jasmine Jacob has expanded her network.

5. *Finding a mentor*. The aspiring woman seeks out successful women who can help her become a woman of excellence. A mentor gives counsel and guidance in a particular field. She encourages and strengthens, listens and assists. Usually a mentor is an older woman who can share the benefits of her experience.

6. *Sharing what she knows*. The successful woman will look for ways to share her expertise with someone else. She looks for opportunities to teach, share, write, lead a seminar, or simply talk with a friend over a cup of herb tea. In finding ways to share what she knows, she expands her network and finds her talents growing as well.

Women Need Women

In our churches we need women who can encourage other women. In our conferences we need women who can lead others to become effective workers for God. We need women who will go out from their homes to make disciples of other women. As we help other women to become a success, we are obeying the suggestion of Paul: "Let the aged women . . . teach the young women" (Titus 2:3, 4).

The General Conference has recognized the need for women to become leaders for God. For this purpose we have the Office of Women's Ministries. Its purpose is to nurture and train Adventist women, helping them be all that God has gifted them to become.

Women need women. There are many hurting women in our churches and communities: grieving women, abused women, battered women, forsaken women, addicted women, lonely women. There are so many needs, needs that only another woman can fill.

"The Lord has a work for women as well as for men. They may take their places in His work at this crisis, and He will work through them. If they are imbued with a sense of their duty, and labor under the influence of the Holy Spirit, they will have just the self-possession required for this time. The Saviour will reflect upon these self-sacrificing women the light of His countenance, and will give them a power that exceeds that of men. They can do in families a work that men cannot do, a work that reaches the inner life. They can come close to the hearts of those whom men cannot reach. Their labor is needed" (Ellen G. White, *Welfare Ministry,* p. 145).

Wonderful things happen when women begin to support one another. Miracles occur when women begin to expand their networks. A case in point is Anne Sullivan.

Annie's Network

A gray-haired nurse sat on the cold stone floor outside of Annie's room and opened a brown paper sack. She removed a brownie and held it out to the teenage girl huddled in a corner. "Come, Annie, see what nurse has brought you."

Annie made no move to take the food. Her sightless eyes stared straight ahead.

"Hopeless!" the doctors had said.

"Nothing but a wild creature!" nurses had agreed. "She's got nobody, nobody in the world." Annie's network was empty.

She's got to have somebody, the gray-haired nurse decided, and so she set out to become a part of little, wild Annie's network. "I wish you'd talk to me," the nurse sighed. "I know life has been hard on you. First your mother died when you were 8, and then two years later your father deserted you. Then you and Jimmie had to come to this poorhouse. That was tough."

But Annie had decided to shut out the cruel world. She

wanted no one in her personal network. She held her arms tightly to herself and turned away toward the wall.

"Then to top it off, your brother died and you went blind. No wonder you kicked and screamed so much that they put you here. I'd have been mad too. I know you're not crazy, like they think. You're just hurting real bad. I love you, Annie, and I'll come back tomorrow to talk."

Although Annie refused to talk, she ate the brownie after the nurse left. The older woman's love kept her coming back day after day. And every Thursday she brought brownies. Little by little, Annie began to respond to the nurse's kindness and support. She started to smile and talk. She stopped kicking and screaming.

The old nurse was now part of Annie's personal network. And soon others joined the network of friends. The doctors noticed the change in Annie and decided she didn't need isolation anymore. They sent her to a school for the blind run by Alexander Graham Bell, and her network grew to include other blind children and also teachers and doctors who worked with the blind. People in her enlarged world taught her sign language. They helped her get an operation that restored her sight.

As Annie's network expanded, she learned much from her new friends. Then through Dr. Bell she got a call to teach a 6-year-old girl in Tuscumbia, Alabama. In going to Alabama, Annie expanded her network even further.

That 6-year-old was Helen Keller, blind, deaf, and dumb—and as uncontrollable as a wild animal. Little by little, Annie helped Helen expand her personal network to include the pastor and many others in the community. She encouraged Helen to go to college and get a degree. With Annie's help, Helen's network grew until it included presidents, prime ministers, kings, queens, teachers, and famous people all around the world.

Once Queen Victoria of England, while pinning England's highest award for a foreigner on Helen Keller, asked, "How do you account for your remarkable accomplishments in life? How do you explain the fact that even though you were both blind and deaf, you were able to accomplish so much?''

Without hesitation Helen Keller gave tribute to her mentor. ''If it had not been for my teacher, Anne Sullivan, the name of Helen Keller would have remained unknown.''

The old nurse and Anne Sullivan are examples of the kind of supportive woman I'd like to be.

Rate Yourself

On a scale of 1 to 5 (5 being the very best) rate yourself in your use of the following methods of expanding your network.

1. The successful woman seeks new experiences, learns new skills, and enjoys gaining new information.

1   2   3   4   5

2. The woman of excellence risks connecting with people and organizations.

1   2   3   4   5

3. The successful woman shows belonging to a group by participating, cooperating, and expressing enthusiasm.

1   2   3   4   5

4. The woman who is a winner exhibits specializing. She seeks a need, then tries to fill it.

1   2   3   4   5

5. The woman of excellence finds a mentor to help her succeed.

1   2   3   4   5

6. The successful woman looks for ways to share her expertise with others.

1   2.   3   4   5

Personal Growth Exercises

1. Think of the biggest achievement of your life. Write that achievement at the top of a sheet of paper. Under it, make a list of all the people who helped make it possible. Then take a moment to thank the Lord for the network of friends who helped you achieve.

2. Draw a small circle in the center of a sheet of paper. Surround it with five concentric circles. Let each circle stand for one level of your personal network. Label the circles. Write the names of at least three people who fit into each circle.

3. Read the stories of Ruth and Esther, looking for examples of how they made use of the six success skills given in this chapter: experience doing, risk linking, show belonging, exhibit specializing, find a mentor, share what you know. Using the six skills as headings, make an outline of each woman's life, giving as many examples of each skill as you can find.

4. Draw two diagrams of concentric circles as you did in exercise 2. Label one "Ruth's Network" and the other "Esther's Network." Try to fit all the people in each story into one of the network levels. Think about how each woman's network expanded success.

5. Make a list of women who have served as your mentors. What is one thing you learned from each woman?

6. Make a list of women for whom you have been mentor or coach in some aspect of life. What did they learn from you?

7. For a period of time ask God to lead you to a woman whom He sees you could serve as a support, with whom you could share something God has taught you.

8. Buy a small loose-leaf notebook. Use one page for each woman you are seeking to support. Write brief notes about that woman's needs as you discover them. Use the notebook as a guide for your intercessory prayer time. Write in answers to prayer as you receive them.

Success Principle

We cannot be a success in life alone. What we become depends a great deal on the people in our personal networks.

For Additional Reading

Barnes, Emilie. *Things Happen When Women Care: Hospitality and Friendship in Today's Busy World*. Harvest House.

Brestin, Dee. *The Friendships of Women*. Victor.

Boyer, Pam. *Forever Friends: Cultivating Close Relationships*. Harvest House.

Kraft, Vickie. *Women Mentoring Women*. Moody Press.

CHAPTER SIX

A Happy Woman

IANCA ROTHSCHILD had every reason to be bitter. In 1939, just before her sixteenth birthday, war broke out in Poland. Six years later she was the only survivor from a family of 43. All the others had died in concentration camps.

She suffered much at the hands of her captors: broken ribs, a broken wrist, a mangled leg, and a back damaged when a Nazi guard stomped on her with his heavy boots. Today she still wears a brace because of that beating.

After that experience she ran outside during an air raid and prayed for a bomb to kill her. When she survived, she began to wonder what purpose God had for her life.

Back inside, she opened a book and read: "We have a right to the joy of giving so others may receive. We can give material things, we can give moral support, we can give a friendly ear, and best of all, we can give love."

Bianca realized she had two choices. She could spend the rest of her life feeling sorry for herself, harboring a spirit of hate and bitterness, or she could choose the way of love and kindness, looking away from herself to the needs of others.

That night she prayed, "Dear God! Help me through this terrible ordeal, and I vow to give myself in a true and loving spirit."

After the war she immigrated to the United States and ended up living in a condominium complex in San Diego. It was there she found a very special way to love.

Most of the residents in this particular condominium are elderly and often need a little bit of sunshine. Whenever anyone is in the hospital or laid up at home, Bianca sends a cheery get well card. Each one she signs, "The Sunshine Lady." Over the years dozens of people have received a card from this woman with the sunny temperament.

A neighbor commented, "There's something wrong with her back, but it never seems to have any effect on her happy disposition."

They don't know about her battle with bitterness and despair that night in the concentration camp. They only see the results.

Bianca Rothschild is an example of the happy, positive woman I want to be, one able to conquer her negative emotions.

Like a Ship at Sea

Sometimes I feel like a ship's captain struggling to keep my vessel afloat on a stormy sea. The circumstances of the moment hang over me like a dense fog. Have I no control? Have I no choice but to drift aimlessly, at the mercy of the elements? Why do I so often get off course? What keeps me from being the happy, positive woman I want to be?

I'd like to suggest that negative emotions are the winds that blow us off course. Problems at home, difficulties at church, and temptations on the job threaten to dash us against the rocks. Like an oil tanker broken apart on the rocks, we are torn open by our troubles, spilling out angry, hurtful words.

What can we do to stay on course in spite of the difficult circumstances that come our way? How can we prevent the expensive clean-up process that follows the spilling out of our negative emotions? In my search for help to cope with negative emotions, I have discovered four biblical principles.

1. God understands our feelings. Jesus sympathizes with me. He truly can feel what I feel. Although no one else may understand my struggle, He does.

"For we have not an high priest which cannot be touched with the feeling of our infirmities; but was in all points tempted like as we are, yet without sin" (Heb. 4:15).

Jesus can be touched by my feelings, for He faced similar trials. Jesus suffered emotional pain, injustice, rejection, loneliness, and grief. He longed for human acceptance. He too cried. As David Seamands points out in his book *Healing for Damaged Emotions*, Jesus is "the wounded healer" of our pain.

The experience of Hagar is an example of God's ability to understand how we feel. He heard her cries in the desert. He saw each tear she shed. He understood her feelings of despair, pain, loneliness, and abandonment.

"His heart of love is touched by our sorrows, and even by our utterances of them. . . . No calamity can befall the least of His children, no anxiety harass the soul, no joy cheer, no sincere prayer escape the lips, of which our heavenly Father is unobservant, or in which He takes no immediate interest" (Ellen G. White, *Steps to Christ,* p. 100).

2. Contact with God transforms negative emotions. "To appoint unto them that mourn in Zion, to give unto them beauty for ashes, the oil of joy for mourning, the garment of praise for the spirit of heaviness" (Isa. 61:3).

Jesus has a balm for every emotional sore spot. He can give us joy for our depression and peace for our pain. He can give love for our hatred and relief for our bitterness. He has hope for our despair and acceptance to apply to our low self-worth.

When her husband took another wife, Hannah must have felt rejection and then jealousy as that woman proved fertile.

She no doubt felt discouraged and depressed, perhaps even bitter. There might have been guilt. It must have been hard for Hannah to visit the tabernacle. She couldn't have felt like going out among people. But she made the effort to meet God, and her sorrow was turned into joy.

3. *God can supply our emotional needs.* "My God shall supply all your need" (Phil. 4:19).

Minirth and Meier in their book *Happiness Is a Choice* list 12 needs that we all share: air, food, water, stimulation, sex, love, self-worth, power, aggression, comfort, security, and relief for psychic tension.

God wants to meet *all* our needs, the emotional as well as the physical. He can supply us with love, acceptance, comfort, and security. He can provide us with strength to face a problem and relief from the tensions of life.

The woman at the well had tried to supply her emotional needs through a succession of men, only to be disappointed. In Christ she found the needs of her heart supplied.

Bev's husband left her with three children to raise alone. She claimed the promise of Isaiah 54:5, and Christ became as a husband to her. In Him she found all the comfort, strength, security, and happiness she needed.

Georgia, suffering the effects of a dysfunctional family, tried to fill her need for love with church work and community activities. She chaired the music committee, played the organ, helped the homeless, led the youth, and taught a Bible class. When that didn't meet her emotional needs, she turned to drugs. For eight years she struggled with addiction while attending church every week. No one suspected her pain. It wasn't until she experienced God's unconditional love that Georgia found release from her negative emotions.

4. *Feelings follow actions.* "And when they began to sing and to praise, the Lord set ambushments against the children of Ammon, Moab, and mount Seir, which were come against Judah; and they were smitten" (2 Chron. 20:22).

The Israelites must not have felt victorious when faced

with the superior forces of the enemy, but they went to battle singing praises. The feeling of victory followed their action of victory.

Linda struggled with feelings of bitterness toward someone who had criticized her severely. She asked the Lord to replace that bitterness with love. However, the feeling didn't come until she stepped out in faith and acted as though she loved the woman who had wronged her. She sent her a little gift. Whenever she saw her, Linda greeted her with a warm hug and kind words. Miraculously the bitterness was replaced with love. The positive feelings followed Linda's positive actions.

Positive Strategies

One of the most difficult years of my life was the year I taught in Kitchener, Ontario, so that I could be available to help our adopted East Indian children adapt to life in North America while my husband returned to his work in Bangalore, India. We were separated for 10 months, and the loneliness I felt was terrible. I was neither widowed nor divorced, so no one seemed to understand how alone and helpless I felt. During that period of emotional pain six things helped me cope with negative feelings.

1. Nature. I walked for hours in the woods, identifying wildflowers and birds. I talked aloud to God on those walks. I felt the closeness of His presence, and He did indeed fill my emotional needs during those times of communion in nature.

2. Singing. I would often sing my prayers. Using familiar tunes, I made up my own words that expressed my heartache and pain, my hope and thanksgiving. I made new verses to fit my concerns of the moment. Though I have no musical talent, there was something about the use of music that opened my heart to God's love. I often cried as I sang, so real was my sense of God's presence, of His concern for my needs and the needs of my family.

3. Helping others. I visited people in nursing homes. I helped with church duties. I discovered in the process that others had a lot worse problems to deal with than I did. In giving my attention to the needs of others, my own pain was eased.

4. Exercise. It's hard to feel down after a long, brisk walk in the sunshine. I remember once when I was angry with my mother-in-law. I went for a six-mile walk. By the time I returned, the anger had been replaced with understanding.

5. Learning. It's surprising what enrolling in a class or reading a book on a new subject can do for negative emotions. Learning something new takes the focus away from our problems and gives us something interesting to talk about besides our difficulties. I made good use of the library that year!

6. Journaling. Although I have been journaling on a regular basis for only six years, this is a method I have often turned to during times of crisis. By writing out my prayers I have found emotional release and a means of sorting through my conflicting feelings. There is something about seeing a frustration or anxiety on paper that makes it manageable. Insight and strength come as I explore my feelings before God on paper.

Corrie's Experience

Whenever Corrie thought of her guard at Ravensbrück, a deep, dark bitterness churned in her stomach. "I hate that man," she said. "I can never forgive him."

"You must forgive him," the Lord said to her in the quietness of her daily devotions. "If you do not forgive men their sins, your father will not forgive yours."

Although she had no feelings of forgiveness in her heart, she decided to obey God and try. She wrote a letter that said, "What you meant to be harmful, God used for my good."

But writing a letter and seeing him in person were two different matters. It was two years after the letter that she saw him. She had spoken to a large crowd, and he had come forward to speak to her. Instantly she recognized that face. A wave of horror passed over her.

He stuck out his hand, "A fine message, Fräulein! How good it is to know, as you say, all our sins are at the bottom of the sea!"

"You were a guard at Ravensbrück," Corrie heard herself say. "I remember you. Do you remember me?"

"I don't remember you," he replied. "There were so many. But I have become a Christian since then. I know that God has forgiven me for the cruel things I did there, but I would like to hear it from your lips as well. Fräulein, will you forgive me?"

Suddenly Corrie realized that she had no control over those emotions of anger, hatred, and bitterness. How could this man expect all those horrid memories to disappear? She looked into her heart and saw no forgiveness there.

Jesus, help me! she prayed silently. *I can lift my hand. I can do that much. You supply the feeling.*

Woodenly, mechanically, she thrust her hand into the one stretched out to her. And as she did, an incredible thing took place. She said, "The current started in my shoulders, raced down my arm, sprang into our joined hands. And then this healing warmth seemed to flood my whole being, bringing tears to my eyes."

"I forgive you, brother!" she cried. "With all my heart, I forgive you."

Rate Yourself

Below are a list of negative emotions. Put a check beside those that you are feeling now or have felt recently.

___Frustration	___Anger	___Rage
___Envy	___Jealousy	___Hatred
___Pessimism	___Fear	___Anxiety
___Self-pity	___Discouragement	___Depression
___Regret	___Shame	___Guilt
___Grief	___Bitterness	___Low self-worth

Following is a list of positive emotions. Which ones do you feel in particular need of at the present time?

___Love	___Understanding	___Compassion
___Peace	___Forgiveness	___Acceptance
___Joy	___Patience	___Tolerance
___Trust	___Tranquility	___Security
___Happiness	___Expectancy	___Hope
___Strength	___Power	___Self-control
___High self-worth	___Assertiveness	___Adventure

Personal Growth Exercises

1. You will need a notebook. At the top of each page write one of the negative emotions you checked above. Under it explore that emotion. Why do you feel that way? What do you perceive as being the causes for that feeling?

2. List some strategies you could use to cope with each negative feeling. What positive feeling would you like to have in its place? Present each of these negative emotions to God.

3. Using a concordance, search for Bible verses that promise the very positive emotions you need. Look up the promises in various versions. Using 3″ x 5″ cards, write out at least one promise for each positive emotion. Put these at strategic places where you can read them often.

4. Try paraphrasing Bible promises. Write out the promise, inserting your name in the verse at appropriate places. What message is God trying to give to you in that verse? Write out what you hear Him saying to you.

5. The Psalms are full of references to emotions. Read through a psalm, underlining negative emotions in one color and positive emotions in a contrasting color.

6. Choose an incident from the life of a Bible woman. Read of her experience in Scripture and in the Spirit of Prophecy. Try to imagine the emotions she was experiencing in that situation. How would you have felt if you had been in her shoes? How did she deal with her negative emotions? What can you learn from her experience?

7. Read the last chapter of *Steps to Christ*, "Rejoicing in the Lord." Make a list of positive actions we can take when dealing with negative emotions.

Success Principle
With God's help we can choose to exchange negative emotions for positive ones.

For Additional Reading
Dobson, James. *Emotions: Can You Trust Them?* Regal Books.

Minirth, Frank, and Meier, Paul. *Happiness Is a Choice.* Baker Book House.

Minirth, Frank, and Meier, Paul. *Love Is a Choice.*

Minirth, Frank, and Meier, Paul. *Love Is a Choice Workbook.*

O'Conner, Karen. *When Spending Takes the Place of Feeling: Women Who Spend Too Much and Don't Know Why.* Thomas Nelson.

Rinehart, Paula. *Perfect Every Time: When Becoming the Woman You Thought You Should Be Is Hurting the Woman You Are.* NavPress.

Seamonds, David. *Healing for Damaged Emotions.* Victor Books.

Shaw, Luck. *Life Path: Personal and Spiritual Growth Through Journal Writing.* Multnomah.

Shepperson, Vance L. and Shepperson, Bethel Joy. *Tracks in the Sand: Your Guide to Recovery Journaling.* Thomas Nelson.

CHAPTER SEVEN
....

A Loving Woman

MIRIAM ADENEY needed a baby-sitter for six weeks. A job placement service sent her Ashraf, an Iranian mother of two children.

Ashraf's husband had promised to send her money, but after she arrived in the United States he discovered he couldn't get his funds out of Iran. Here she was, a woman who spoke little English, alone in a strange land with two children to support.

When the six weeks were over, Miriam felt she just couldn't let Ashraf go without trying to help her get another job. Ashraf had started reading a Farsi Bible given her by her language tutor. "The story of Jesus is so beautiful," she told Miriam. Now it was Christmas, and Miriam felt compelled to help.

"Why do you bother?" friends asked. "It's really not your responsibility to get Ashraf a job."

"But I just can't push her out to starve," Miriam insisted. "I know I don't have time, but I have to do something to help."

Miriam got several newspapers and began looking at the

"Baby-sitter Wanted" ads. Eventually she found a job for Ashraf.

Meanwhile Ashraf continued reading her Farsi Bible. As a result she accepted Jesus as her Saviour. She phoned her husband in Iran and received permission to be baptized.

Of course Miriam attended her baptism. So did her language instructor. So did other friends who had welcomed her into their church and into their homes.

In her testimony Ashraf said, "I am being baptized today because of the love of Christians." She smiled at Miriam, her language teacher, and other friends. "Through them I have discovered what a beautiful, loving person Jesus Christ is."

That's the kind of woman I want to be—so loving and compassionate that others will be drawn to Jesus Christ and His church. How can I communicate love?

Love Listens

"Everyone should be quick to listen, slow to speak" (James 1:19, NIV). Listening is one way to show love. Most of us are not good listeners. When someone else is talking we are thinking of our own stories to tell.

Books have been written about how to listen, but we can boil it down to three basic principles: (1) use the body language of a listener, (2) use open questions, (3) use reflective listening.

1. Body language. Experts tell us that 90 percent of our communication is through body language. We often say one thing, but really mean something else, and our body language shows it.

A good listener faces the person who is speaking squarely, shoulder to shoulder, face-to-face. She maintains an open body posture, arms and legs uncrossed. She leans forward slightly toward the speaker and maintains eye contact.

Eye level is also important. To stand or sit above the person talking puts one in the position of authority, not the position of a friendly listener. Even my golden retriever, Matt, knows this much. When he meets a dog on the trail, he lies low, allowing the other the position of dominance.

For many years my husband has been in conference work, speaking at a different church each Sabbath. I used to feel bad that I had to sit alone. Why was everyone so unfriendly?

One day I took notice of my body language. I was sitting at the end of the pew, my arms and legs crossed. By my choice of the end position and my body language I was unconsciously saying to everyone, "Stay away. I don't want you to sit with me."

I moved down several spaces, sat in an open, relaxed position, and smiled as people looked my way. Soon the row filled up on each side of me. Body language really does make a difference!

2. Open questions. Open questions accomplish more than closed questions. Closed questions ask for facts. They have one right answer. Closed questions are conversation stoppers. Too many closed questions make people feel as though they were on trial.

Open questions ask for reasons, opinions, thoughts, feelings, and explanations. They allow the other person to express herself in any way she desires. Open questions are nonrestricting and nonthreatening. Open questions allow the other person to share while you listen.

3. Reflective listening. The speaker has an idea in her mind. She chooses words, putting her message into code. We receive the coded message, but must then try to figure out the real message the speaker wants to convey with those words. Often the message is quite different than what the words indicate.

Good listeners check back with the speaker to make sure they got the correct message. A perception check shows we really care about the person. We want to understand her.

Sharon says, "Shut off the radio."

Brenda thinks, *She can't stand my type of music*.

However, that may not be Sharon's message at all. She

could mean *I'm trying to study, so I need quiet.* Or *I need your attention. We should talk.* Or *I'm annoyed by what you said last night and I want to pick a fight with you.*

Love listens, hearing not only the words but the feeling behind the words. Love takes time to check to see if the message received is the one given.

When My Husband Listened

One Sunday afternoon my husband, Ron, gave me a lesson in how to listen. We were sitting in our living room when our neighbor two doors down drove in from church with his new wife. His first wife had left him with two hyperactive boys. Now he had a new wife with three children of her own. They looked so happy piling out of the car that day.

"Tim and his new wife really look happy," Ron commented.

"Yeah," I said. "He's probably made all sorts of promises to her, and she'll wake up one of these days and realize he hasn't kept them."

Ron's recent training in listening nudged him to say, "Are you talking about *their* marriage or *our* marriage?"

After a moment I admitted, "I guess I was talking about our marriage."

"What do you mean?" he asked.

"You don't want to hear," I answered. After all, I'd tried for many years to tell him how I felt, and he hadn't heard me.

"Yes, I do want to hear," he insisted, putting down his newspaper. "Try me out."

I talked for two and a half hours, and he listened. It was wonderful! There were tears, and a renewed closeness, the beginning of a new phase in our marriage. This happened because he listened to the feeling and meaning behind my words.

Love Overcomes Roadblocks

We can see this characteristic of love demonstrated in the

contrast between the way the Pharisees treated the woman taken in adultery and the way Christ dealt with her.

The Pharisees came scolding, criticizing, complaining, moralizing, punishing, shaming, and blaming. Instead of communicating love, they erected roadblocks between themselves and her, roadblocks that communicated dislike, unacceptance, and hostility.

Christ dealt with the same woman in a loving manner. He accepted her just as she was, and in that acceptance He gave her the courage she needed to be different. He tore down the roadblocks of unacceptance, and He communicated love.

There are three basic categories of roadblocks: judging, sending solutions, and avoiding the other's concerns.

1. Judging. Judging roadblocks include criticizing, name-calling, diagnosing, labeling, blaming, and shaming. The judging roadblocks make a person feel unaccepted and unacceptable. "Judge not," Jesus said. I must tear down the judging roadblocks if I want to communicate love.

I sat in a Sabbath school class as a visitor. We were sharing blessings and prayer concerns. Another visitor spoke up, "Please pray for my sister who has cancer."

"If she had been following Ellen White's counsels on health, she wouldn't be sick," a dour lady interrupted.

Talking and sharing stopped. We all felt the hurt and unacceptance of that remark.

2. Sending solutions. Sending solutions roadblocks include ordering, commanding, demanding, threatening, preaching, moralizing, interrogating, and advising. These roadblocks cause resistance and resentment. They imply that the other person's judgment is unsound. The other person begins to feel unloved, worthless, and helpless. I must break down the sending solutions roadblocks if I want to communicate love.

3. Avoiding the other's concerns. We avoid the other's concerns by diverting, distracting, arguing, and reassuring, all the things we do to try to get people who are feeling bad to feel

A LOVING WOMAN

better. We change the subject or tell them it's not really so bad and they'll feel better by and by. The use of this type of roadblock communicates our desire to withdraw from another's pain. If I would communicate love, I must overcome the roadblocks.

An Example of Roadblocks

I came home from school one day and said to Ron, "I'm going to quit teaching. I had a terrible day. I'm an awful teacher."

Ron replied, "Stop talking like that. You're a good teacher, and you know it!"

"No, I'm not! I did a lousy job today."

"It's not as bad as you think," he said. "You'll feel better after a good night's rest." And he went out to mow the lawn.

I curled up on the bed and started to cry. He hadn't listened. He hadn't understood how terrible my day had been.

While I was feeling sorry for myself, he was outside thinking about what he had done. He came back inside and tried again.

"Honey," he said above my sobs, "you really did have a terrible day. You feel like you did a lousy job. Nothing went right. You want to quit teaching. It was really bad."

I stopped crying and sat up. He understood! He really cared! Suddenly I felt loved and able to go on.

"Want to tell me about it?" he asked.

"Maybe later." I smiled as I got up and headed for the kitchen. "Right now I think I'll fix supper."

It didn't really matter how awful my day had been, for I had received a communication of love.

Love Is Vulnerable

Jesus gave up His high position to come and be as we are. He became approachable, but at the same time He opened Himself to attack. He made Himself vulnerable, able to be hurt and rejected.

Love strips away our layers of pride and makes us approachable. We become vulnerable, willing to show our humanity. We let others know that we aren't so different than they after all.

It was my first year teaching at Portland Adventist Academy. I barely knew Jan, who taught across the hall. One afternoon I crossed the hall and said, "Jan, I had a bad day. The children were so restless. I feel like I did a terrible job."

"I love it!" Jan responded. "You always look so cool, calm, and collected. It's nice to know you are human like the rest of us." We had a great talk that afternoon, and that was the beginning of a friendship that lasts to this day.

Being open, honest, and human is difficult for many of us Adventist women. We want people to think we have it all together. We smile and put on a brave front when we are hurting inside.

Pat was meeting Gloria, whom she had not seen in years. Gloria welcomed Pat to her home cordially, but with reserve. She sat on the opposite end of the sofa, her legs and arms crossed.

Then Pat took note of her own posture. Her legs and arms were crossed. She smiled, uncrossed her arms and legs, leaned forward and said, "Tell me about your children. How are they doing?"

"Oh, just great!" Gloria said. She looked so poised, so self-assured. "And how are your children, Pat?"

Pat decided to be honest. "To tell you the truth, not so good right now. They've made some wrong choices, and I'm feeling very much a failure as a mother."

As Pat shared openly about her feelings, Gloria uncrossed her arms and legs and moved closer to Pat. Before long she said, "I wasn't being honest with you. I've had similar problems. We're praying for our kids, too. That's all we can do."

As Pat told me later, "What a beautiful time of fellowship

we had—all because I was willing to open up, to become vulnerable!''

Love Encourages

"Let us encourage one another" (Heb. 10:25, NIV).

Voicing our appreciation is the most effective way to encourage someone. It is simply doing what God did for His Son at the Jordan River, speaking words of sincere appreciation. "This is my beloved Son, in whom I am well pleased."

Charlie Blake is an example of what can happen through the power of encouragement. Charlie was known as the "sickest man in Britain." He did nothing all day except sit in a chair. He seldom moved and never talked. An orderly labeled him "Mr. Zero." He hadn't said a word in 30 years.

At this point Dr. Irene Kassorla decided to try the power of affirmation. Every day she visited him. She rewarded any movement or sound with a positive word of appreciation. She said things such as "Good, Mr. Blake" or "I like that sound you're making." After 31 days Charlie was talking, reading the newspaper, and answering questions.

About her use of appreciation Dr. Kassorla says: "The results have been so remarkable that an untrained observer might have wondered if I were administering a potent new drug. But my 'drug' was often little more than presenting warm, caring words."

Words have a tremendous power. A word spoken at the right time can change the whole course of a person's life.

Take, for instance, the case of Larry Crabb, a name on several books in Christian bookstores. While in ninth grade he was called upon to offer prayer during the worship service in his church. He was so nervous that he not only stuttered, but his theology became confused. He thanked the Father for hanging on the cross and praised Christ for bringing the Spirit from the grave.

Finally, Larry managed to say "Amen" and sit down. He knew he'd made a fool of himself, and he vowed never again to pray in public or speak before an audience. As soon as the meeting was finished, Larry darted for the door, but he wasn't fast enough. One of the elders intercepted his flight.

Larry gulped. *Oh, no!* he thought. *Here it comes!*

The elder put an arm on Larry's shoulder and cleared his throat. "Larry, there's one thing I want you to know. Whatever you do for the Lord, I'm behind you 1,000 percent."

Today Larry is a college professor who has a wide public ministry. He often tells the story of that elder's encouragement, but he never tells it without choking up, so powerful was the impact of those few encouraging words.

Rate Yourself

On a scale of 1 to 5, rate yourself on the following ways of communicating love. Five is the best.

1. Love listens not only to the words a person says, but to the meaning and the feeling behind the words.

1   2   3   4   5

2. A good listener faces the speaker, keeps body in an open position, and maintains eye contact.

1   2   3   4   5

3. A good listener asks more open questions than closed questions.

1   2   3   4   5

4. Love overcomes the judging roadblocks.

1   2   3   4   5

5. Love overcomes the sending solutions roadblocks.

1   2   3   4   5

6. Love overcomes the avoiding the other's concerns roadblocks.

1	2	3	4	5

7. Love becomes vulnerable. It makes us open, honest, and human.

1	2	3	4	5

8. Love encourages by voicing appreciation.

1	2	3	4	5

Personal Growth Exercises

1. On the blank beside each statement below, identify the type of roadblock it represents. Is it (1) Judging, (2) Sending solutions, or (3) Avoiding the other's concerns?

_____ That was a stupid thing to say.

_____ You just want to look good.

_____ You'd better do it, or else.

_____ You really ought to try it.

_____ You usually have good judgment.

_____ Stop it right now!

_____ That's just like a man!

_____ You'll feel better tomorrow.

_____ There is only one logical conclusion.

2. Find an opportunity to engage an acquaintance in conversation. Your object is to keep the conversation going for a minimum of four minutes, the length of time it takes to turn an acquaintance into a friend. It is a real challenge for some people to cross the four-minute barrier. Use open questions rather than closed questions.

3. Let today be "Affirmation Day." Find at least 12 people to whom you can voice your honest appreciation. You may do this in person, use the phone, or write a note. At the end of the day make a list of the people you encouraged.

4. Make a "Warm Fuzzies" jar for your home, school room, or office. People write down on slips of paper good

things they notice in other people and drop them in the jar. At the end of the week open the jar and read the compliments out loud to the group.

5. Try an ''Alphabet of Love.'' List the letters of the alphabet vertically on paper. Beside each letter try to think of words that begin with that letter which describe what love is or what love does. (A—Love is affirming, appreciative, etc.)

Success Principle

L—Listening
O—Overcoming roadblocks
V—Vulnerability
E—Encouragement

For Additional Reading

Crabb, Larry. *The Marriage Builder*. Zondervan.

Dillow, Linda. *Creative Counterpart*, revised and updated. Thomas Nelson.

Esau, Truman with Burch, Beverly. *Making Marriage Work: Developing Intimacy With the One You Love*. Victor Books.

Gilbert, Dave, and Bradshaw, Charles. *Too Hurried to Love: Finding Time for the Ones You Love*. Harvest House.

Littauer, Florence. *How to Get Along With Difficult People*. Harvest House.

Luciano, Mark and Meris, Christopher, *If Only He Would Change: What to Do When Your Marriage Is Not What You Thought It Would Be*. Thomas Nelson.

Minirth, Frank and Mary Alice, Newman, Brian and Deborah, Hemfelt, Robert and Susan. *Passages of Marriage*. Thomas Nelson.

Smalley, Gary with Trent, John. *Love Is a Decision*. Word.

CHAPTER EIGHT

An Assertive Woman

MARY MITCHELL SLESSOR, a nineteenth-century missionary in Africa and the first woman magistrate in the British Empire, is one of my heroines. I admire her for her courage. She was a woman who did not run away from a fight with her antagonists, but she stood her ground and faced each situation calmly, knowing exactly what she wanted. Mary Slessor was an assertive woman.

An example of her response to conflict was an incident that took place when she was 16 years old. She had started a Sunday school class for children in the slums of Dundee, Scotland. A gang of boys decided to put a stop to it.

The boys surrounded Mary, and the leader began swinging a lead weight on a string in circles that came increasingly closer to her head. All the while the boys shouted, "Leave us alone if you don't want to get hurt! We don't want any of your goody-goody teachings! You'd better stop that Bible class!"

Mary, slight of build and with strawberry-blonde hair cut short, was quite a contrast to the street boys who surrounded her. No fear showed in her blue eyes as she stood there straight and tall, never wavering. The lead weight swung within a fraction of an inch of her head, then the leader's hand dropped, and the weight clattered onto the pavement.

"No good, lads," he said. "She's game. We can't frighten her." Some of the toughs slunk away, but others joined her class.

Years later in Africa Mary showed the same intrepid spirit. There was a custom that if a person died through an accident, it was thought that an enemy had killed him or her. All suspects were forced to eat a poisonous bean. They believed that only the guilty would die. On arriving in one village, Mary saw 12 men and women chained in a compound, where they waited to eat the poisonous bean.

"You must not do this," Mary said.

"Yes," the villagers shouted. "We will do it."

Mary planted her small frame at the gateway to the compound and declared, "I will not move from here until you set them all free." She held her ground for several days until the men grew tired of struggling with her. The prisoners were finally set free, and a cow was sacrificed at the burial instead of the people.

I don't expect to face a crowd of hoodlums or have to withstand angry village chiefs, but I know that inevitably I will face conflict in my life. Friends sometimes annoy. Occasionally my husband is frustrating. Teenagers have a way of getting my dander up. Sometimes my boss does things that upset me. Even strangers bring me into conflict when they push ahead in a queue.

How can we handle conflict when people become difficult?

Three Ways to Handle Conflict

There are three ways to handle conflict. We can fight. We can run away. But a better way is to focus on the problem, face it, and resolve it. Fight. Flight. Focus.

It is evening at the Joneses' home. Heather and Steve have

just finished supper. Heather, an elementary teacher, has the laundry to do as well as report cards to finish before bedtime.

Steve says, "Let's go for a walk."

Heather feels instant frustration. She can't possibly do all three activities. How might she handle the conflict she feels?

Fight. "How come you always wait until I have a million things to do before asking me to go for a walk? You're so inconsiderate. Sometimes I wonder why I even married you!"

Flight. "Sure, honey, whatever you say." Heather goes on the walk but silently seethes, lags behind, and complains about how fast Steve walks. She stays up until 1:00 a.m. to finish her work and goes to bed feeling greatly persecuted.

Focus. "Honey, your wanting me to go on a walk right now really frustrates me because I want to be with you, but I have to do the laundry and finish my report cards. I don't see how I can do all that and go for a walk too."

Focus is always the best response to conflict. It brings the conflict into the open. It expresses feelings, but does not blame. It allows the other person freedom to help resolve the conflict. Fight and flight messages only make conflict worse. Focus messages make room for a solution.

Biblical Examples

The story of Queen Esther illustrates these three ways to handle conflict.

Fight. Haman decided to fight Mordecai. He chose force to deal with the difficult person in his life. He built a gallows on which to hang the man he hated.

Flight. Haman's relationship with the king is an example of flight. When the king sent him to lead Mordecai through the streets, he meekly submitted to the king's wish, all the time hating what he had to do.

Focus. Esther used the focus message in her relationships. She confronted the king. She asserted herself. She said, "King Ahasuerus, when you make a law to kill all the Jews, I feel threatened, because I also am a Jew." Using the right technique solved Esther's problem and eliminated the conflict.

Modern Conflicts

In a Sabbath school class the people behind you keep talking in a fairly loud voice, distracting you from the lesson. How might you resolve the conflict?

Fight. Turn around and snarl at them, "Don't you have any respect for others? If you want to talk, you should leave!"

Flight. Get up and leave yourself. Try another class. Or just ignore the problem, hoping it will go away. It won't.

Focus. Smile sweetly and say, "Your talking disturbs me because I am unable to hear the teacher."

What about this situation? A school principal makes frequent announcements over the loudspeaker system and interrupts your classroom unnecessarily. How might you handle conflict with your boss?

Fight. "What kind of stupid jerk are you, sending messages over the intercom at all times of day? Can't you ever get organized enough to give them all at once? Why don't you copy your stupid announcement?" Not a good choice if you value your job.

Flight. Say nothing. Ignore the problem. Things won't get any better and probably will get worse.

Focus. Ask for an appointment. Tell him, "When you make frequent announcements I feel frustrated because it interrupts my lessons. It is difficult to regain the students' attention, and I don't cover what I need to cover.

How to Give a Focus Message

By now it is plain that a focus message is smarter than fight and flight messages. Exactly how do we go about giving a focus message? What ingredients should a focus message have?

Describe the behavior. It should give a nonjudgmental description of the behavior that is upsetting to you. Do not blame or call names. Simply state the problem clearly in an objective manner.

State your feelings. Tell how the behavior makes you feel. Disclose your feelings. Be as accurate as possible. Don't say you are a little upset if very angry is how you really feel.

Show the effect. Give a clear statement of the concrete and tangible effect the behavior has on you. This rules out focusing on someone's choice of hairstyle when it really has no effect on your life except that you dislike it.

Do not give the solution to the problem. Give the other individual freedom to do whatever he or she wishes about the problem.

If someone does not accept your focus message, but argues and defends himself or herself, or calls names, what do you do?

The important thing is to stay in control of the situation. Wait until the person is finished. Try reflective listening skills. Let him or her know that you heard how he or she feels about it. Then repeat your focus message calmly. Keep focusing on the problem. Do not shift to a counterattack on the person.

The Sermon on the Mount

I believe that this concept of taking control of a conflict situation, instead of letting it control you, is what Jesus was trying to teach us in the Sermon on the Mount. He tells us to turn the other cheek, go two miles instead of one, and give more than is asked of us. Isn't this asking us to be a doormat, allowing people to walk all over us? How can we reconcile these commands with facing conflict and focusing on the problem?

I believe that Jesus is saying, "Don't fight when you come into conflict with difficult people." He is telling us, "Don't meekly submit to injustice. Don't run away from conflict." He is saying, "Stand and face the person. Confront him or her with your need to control your own life. Take charge of the situation."

That's exactly what you do when you say, "OK, if you want me to go one mile, I'll make the decision here. I'll go two miles. Do you want my coat? I can do better than that. I'll give you my cloak also."

The Christian way of dealing with interpersonal conflict is not fight. It is not flight. It is confrontation and focus.

Vision of an Iceberg

Ellen White was not by nature a bold, assertive person. She shrunk from the limelight and did not seek conflict. However, she handled it well when it came her way.

In 1903 a conflict was brewing in Battle Creek. The General Conference brethren refused to print Dr. John Harvey Kellogg's book *The Living Temple* because of its erroneous doctrine about the nature of Christ. Dr. Kellogg then published it on his own.

Ellen White received a copy of the offensive book but put it on a shelf unread. One day her son came to her, much troubled about the controversy the book had stirred up.

"Mother, you ought to read at least some parts of the book, that you may see whether they are in harmony with the light that God has given you," he insisted.

Getting the unread book from the shelf, he sat down beside Ellen, and together they read the preface and the first chapter. Leafing through the book they read other paragraphs. The errors were very clear.

That day Ellen had three choices. She could return the book to the shelf and ignore it. But flight was not Ellen's way. Neither did she want to fight with Dr. Kellogg. She chose to focus on the problem, to face it squarely, explaining clearly to Dr. Kellogg and church leaders what she objected to, the effect of publishing the book, then leaving them the freedom to respond however they chose.

For several nights she couldn't sleep, so concerned was she about this conflict. Then one night, about 1:00 in the morning, she had a vision of a ship in a heavy fog. She wrote:

"Suddenly the lookout cried, 'Iceberg just ahead!' There, towering high above the ship, was a gigantic iceberg. An authoritative voice cried out, 'Meet it!' There was not a moment's hesitation. It was a time for instant action. The engineer put on full steam, and the man at the wheel steered the ship straight into the iceberg. With a crash she struck the ice. There was a fearful shock, and the iceberg broke into many pieces, falling with a noise like thunder to the deck. The passengers were violently shaken by the force of the collision, but no lives were lost. The vessel was injured, but not beyond repair."

She continued: "I had my orders. I had heard the words, like a voice from our Captain, 'Meet it!' I knew what my duty was, and that there was not a moment to lose" (*Selected Messages*, book 1, pp. 205, 206).

She got out of bed and began writing, focusing on the problem, making it clear where she stood. God gave Ellen White the courage to face a difficult situation, to be assertive in focusing on the problem at hand. My problems may not be as serious or as far-reaching in scope, but He can give me similar strength to deal with my conflicts.

His promises are sure. "Fear thou not; for I am with thee: be not dismayed; for I am thy God: I will strengthen thee; yea, I will help thee" (Isa. 41:10). "I will be with thee: I will not fail thee, nor forsake thee" (Joshua 1:5).

Rate Yourself—Assertive Skills

Rate yourself on the following assertive skills. One means you have low satisfaction with your skill in that area. Five means you are completely satisfied with your performance of that skill.

1. Use feeling talk. You are comfortable in giving your personal feelings about a subject.

1   2   3   4   5

2. *Talk about yourself.* You are able to share your accomplishments with others.

1   2   3   4   5

3. *Make greeting talk.* You can initiate a conversation without apology or embarrassment.

1   2   3   4   5

4. *Accept compliments.* You can accept compliments graciously instead of disagreeing with them, or playing them down.

1   2   3   4   5

5. *Disagree when necessary.* You do not pretend to agree just to keep peace. You disagree graciously, but clearly.

1   2   3   4   5

6. *Ask for clarification.* Rather than being confused about what someone has said, or directions they have given, you ask him or her to restate or explain.

1   2   3   4   5

7. *Speak up for your rights.* You do not let others take advantage of you when you feel put upon. You can say no without feeling guilty. You can ask to be treated with fairness, as when someone cuts the queue. You can register complaints calmly.

1   2   3   4   5

8. *Avoid justifying yourself.* You are comfortable with your values and don't have to justify your actions and feelings.

1   2   3   4   5

Personal Growth Exercises

1. Practice making focus messages. For each situation below write a focus message. Example:

86

Behavior: You don't clean the counter after making snacks.

Feelings: I feel very annoyed.

Effects: Because it makes more work for me.

A. Someone uses your car and doesn't refill the gas tank.

B. Someone is frequently late picking you up from work.

C. Your assistant, who promised to do something on Sabbath morning, doesn't show up, leaving you holding the bag.

2. Think of some current conflicts you are experiencing. Write out some possible focus messages you could use in dealing with them. Practice those statements.

3. Make a list of feeling words. Try for 100. Rate them as either strong or weak feeling. In focus messages it is important to state correctly the degree of feeling.

Success Principle
The secret of conflict resolution is not fight, or flight, but focus.

For Additional Reading

Smalley, Gary, and Trent, John. *The Language of Love*. Focus on the Family Publishing.

Wright, H. Norman. *How to Speak Your Spouse's Language*. Revell.

Wright, H. Norman. *Caring Enough to Confront*.

CHAPTER NINE

An Organized Woman

TWENTY-ONE-year-old Emilie Barnes had reason to feel stressed out. She had two toddlers of her own plus three of her brother's children to look after since his wife had left him.

One afternoon she put the children to bed for a nap and then lay down to rest herself. She fell asleep and was awakened sometime later by little Keri. The child was covered with red paint! Drops of red led to the neighbor's yard, where there was an open can of paint. What a mess! Emilie closed the can, cleaned the floor, and bathed Keri.

"Keri! That was a very naughty thing to do!" Emilie scolded. "See how much work it has caused me. You must stay in bed. Do not go near that paint again!"

"OK," Keri said.

Emilie lay back down, exhausted. She was no sooner asleep than Keri toddled back outside. Emilie awoke, sensing something was wrong. She checked the bedroom. No Keri. She ran outside to find her once more in the red paint!

Emilie was reaching the breaking point. "Lord, how can I cope?" she prayed. "You've got to help me. I'm washing and ironing and pottying and diapering and mothering 24 hours a day, and I can't handle it. I've not a minute for myself.''

Amid the turmoil of her mind, she felt God speaking to her, ''Emilie, you could get up early in the morning when the house is quiet. You need to spend some time with Me, committing your day to Me.''

Emilie forced herself to set the alarm at 10 minutes to five each morning. She read her Bible, then prayed. She began presenting Him her ''to-do list'' for the day, asking Him to make her the mother that He wanted her to be, to give her time to do what needed to be done, to supply more hours in her day.

Emilie started to get organized. She enrolled the children to help with chores. She kept a marketing list on the refrigerator door. She set about to organize her closets, drawers, and garage. By the time her children were off to college, she was ready to begin a ministry of helping young mothers get organized. She calls her seminars ''More Hours in My Day.''

Emilie Barnes is the kind of organized woman I would like to be. Everything in her house is boxed, filed, or charted. There is a place for everything, and everything is in its place.

Her garage looks like I would like mine to look. There are rows of numbered boxes, cross-referenced into files. She can find anything she needs within minutes. She doesn't go searching through 20 boxes to find a stuffed lamb used in a Christmas pageant five years ago. She knows just which box to open!

This chapter contains ideas I have gleaned from Emilie and other organized people. I have included 10 tools for organizing time and 10 tips for organizing space. They are all methods I have tried, and I know that they work. They are ideas that have helped me work smarter, not harder.

Organizing My Time

Tool 1: No. No! I cannot do everything. I am not a wonder woman. I take time to evaluate requests and do only those I really want to do, those that fit with my priorities. I am learning to say no nicely, and mean it. The woman of excellence knows that she must say no to the good so that she can say yes to the best.

Tool 2: To-do list. I could not live without my to-do list. Sometimes I star the "must-do" items. At times I group types of activities together: phone calls, appointments, projects, errands, chores, and shopping list. I make lists, then lists of lists. The time it takes to do this is worth it. I use 3″ x 5″ index cards for my lists. They don't get lost as easily as pieces of paper and are easy to work with.

Tool 3: Deadlines. I give myself a time when something should be done, and then I try to meet my self-imposed deadline. Sometimes I set a timer and race the timer to see how quickly I can finish a group of routine chores.

The average stay-at-home woman spends 55 hours a week on housekeeping tasks. However, the average working woman spends only 26 hours a week on the same tasks. My goal is to cut down that average even more. I want the extra time to do what I really want to do, things such as writing, birding, antique shopping, hiking, and reading.

Tool 4: Rewards. I reward myself for projects completed. I tell myself things like "Dorothy, get this article written before lunch, and you can go shopping for two hours." "As soon as you get these letters in the mail, Dorothy, you can spent an hour birding at Mill Lake." "Get everything done on your list today, and you can read that new book you got from the library."

Tool 5: The calendar. I couldn't survive without my calendar. Here I list my appointments with the doctor, dentist, vet, hairdresser, as well as speaking appointments, showers, weddings, and the dates writing projects are due. I mark off blocks of time for travel with my husband and time for relaxation and gardening.

My calendar keeps me from overcommitting myself. It makes it easy to say no to requests for my time. My current calendar has the next two weeks blocked off to put the finishing touches on this book. I've said No to several requests for my time as a result.

Tool 6: The journal. My spiritual journal has done more than anything else to help me keep my priorities straight.

What is a spiritual journal? It is not a diary, though it may sometimes tell what I did that day. It is a recording of my thoughts, feelings, and ideas. It often takes the form of a written prayer. Here I keep those messages I feel God is giving me through Scripture and my meditations on nature. I record here my yearly and monthly goals. From time to time I go back to see how I am doing.

Journaling has helped me organize my life and has brought me spiritual renewal. So often our outer world is a mess because our inner world is not organized. I was reaching the burnout point in my life when I discovered journaling. I was a first-class workaholic, going day and night. I was neglecting my inner life, and I wanted to do something about it, but I didn't know what. Journaling turned me around and helped me establish my priorities. It has made a big difference in my ability to juggle the demands of my many roles. Having my inner world in order helps me govern my outer world of activity.

Tool 7: Tickler file. This is something my husband uses that makes our household run more smoothly. He has one file folder for every month of the year. He has another set of folders numbered 1 through 31.

In the monthly folders are reminders of things that must be done that month: bills to be paid, programs to attend, birthdays, and anniversaries. As bills, fliers, and letters come in, he either cares for them then or sticks them in one of the tickler files to be cared for at the correct time.

At the beginning of each month he transfers the items from the current monthly file to the number files, one for each day of that month. The material in the daily tickler file is considered as he makes up his to-do list for that day.

Tool 8: Book of lists. I use a separate journal for my book of lists. Here I keep a list of birthdays and anniversaries for each month, manuscripts sent and payments received, ideas for articles or books, stories and talks given with the date and place, as well as a running list of books I have read.

Once a month I make out all the birthday and anniversary cards, stamp them, and put Post-It note papers on them as to the date they need to be mailed. It's a simple matter then to pick them up on my way out the door.

Tool 9: Message Center. My refrigerator serves as one message center. Lists and reminders are posted all over it, held in place by magnets. Here is a good place for dry-cleaning receipt stubs, photo pickup tabs, and sale notices. My husband and I each have special trays into which we can put mail and messages for each other and know that they will always get read. Another message center is a bulletin board near my desk and computer.

Tool 10: Job cards. Using 3″ by 5″ index cards, I make job cards for projects that need to be done along with specifications I need to remember. These are usually details about speaking appointments and writing projects. They are posted on my bulletin board and thrown away when the task is completed. As I take on new projects, new cards go in place. This string of job cards gives me a feel for the quantity of work I have to do, and also it gives a good feeling each time I am able to finish a project and throw away the card.

Organizing Space

Tip 1: Keys. It really helps to have a special place where all keys go. It saves time searching the house. We have a brass bowl beside our kitchen phone and a cut-glass dish on our dresser for this purpose.

Tip 2: Greeting cards. I buy enough cards in different categories to last six months to a year. These are kept in a labeled box in my office closet. If a wedding or baby announcement comes, I don't have to run to the store to find a card. There is one in my card box, and it is in the mail immediately.

Tip 3: Addresses and phone numbers. I have a loose-leaf address book that travels with me and a Rolodex card file by my desk phone. A short list of much-used phone numbers and emergency numbers on file helps save a lot of time. I don't have to leaf through the yellow pages every time I want to take the dog to the kennel.

Tip 4: Gift box. I have a couple of gift boxes in one cupboard. As I shop I find things on sale that can go into that gift box. I sometimes buy two or three of some books or other neat items. Then they are ready to take as hostess gifts, to give as prizes at a party, or to use whenever I need a small gift. Wedding, shower, and birthday gifts often come out of these boxes.

Tip 5: Warranties and guarantees. I have one drawer designated for these items. I know just where to go when I need one of them.

Tip 6: Kitchen cupboards. It made a big difference when I went through them and took out all the dishes, tins, casseroles, cups, and other items that I never use. These get given away, put in a garage sale, or thrown out. Also, it helps to remove old boxes and tins that haven't been used in six months or more. It helps get rid of the clutter.

Tip 7: Clothes closets. It helps to go through them periodically and take out everything that is the wrong size, color, or style. What is the point of keeping things for years that will never be worn and only take up space? Community Services would be pleased to get these items before they are too old to be useful.

Tip 8: Storage. It has made a world of difference since I have begun to keep little-used items in boxes that I label and keep on shelves. Just a glance at the lower right-hand corner tells what is in the box. I do a number of different seminars, and my visual aids, syllabus masters, and handouts are kept all together in labeled boxes, ready to pull out as needed.

Copy-paper boxes are my favorites for storage because they stack so neatly. Some people collect fruit boxes. Boxes with lids are much easier to deal with than those with flaps. Storage boxes with lids can also be bought in most household supply sections of department stores.

Tip 9: Filing. A filing cabinet is a wise investment. It helps to be able to find clippings, recipes, important papers, and information when you need them. Since I have many different projects I work on from time to time, I use a lot of file boxes that are made to fit inside a regular filing cabinet. I put files for one project in one box, then when I need to work on that I just pull out the whole box of files I will need and keep it on my desk until I am finished with that project.

Tip 10: Sanctuary. It helps to have one place where you keep your Bible, notebook, lesson quarterly, and other items you need for personal devotions. I have found it easier to be regular if I do this at the same spot each day. I keep my materials between bookends on my desk and sit there to read, meditate, and write in my journal. My husband has his corner in his favorite chair in the living room. His materials are kept on the stand beside the chair.

Rate Yourself
Organizational Skills

Rate yourself in each skill. One means you are very poor. Five means you are completely satisfied with how you are doing.

1. Using time effectively. Do you get 60 minutes' work out of each hour?

1   2   3   4   5

2. Planning. Are you able to develop a course of action to accomplish a specific objective?

1   2   3   4   5

3. Controlling paperwork. Do you maintain the flow of

communications: letters, bills, cards, etc., that come to your desk?

1   2   3   4   5

4. Finding things. Can you locate information, tools, and materials quickly when they are needed?

1   2   3   4   5

5. Delegation. Are you able to organize so that others can share in the work and you are not left doing everything yourself?

1   2   3   4   5

6. Pacing your energy use. Are you able to conserve yourself so that you can complete a day without fatigue?

1   2   3   4   5

7. Concentration. Are you able to stick with a given task?

1   2   3   4   5

8. Setting priorities. Do you do the important things first?

1   2   3   4   5

9. Memory. Do you have a system to help you remember important incidents, ideas, plans, or promises?

1   2   3   4   5

10. Clutter control. Are you able to keep a clean, neat house, garage, yard, or work space?

1   2   3   4   5

Personal Growth Exercises

1. Following are specific areas that often need organizing in a home. Circle the areas that need work in your situation.

keys	cards	addresses	phone numbers
gift box	warranties	kitchen	clothes closets
linen closet	garage	storeroom	tools
drawers	filing	books	sanctuary

2. Choose one of the spaces that you circled. What materials do you need to begin working on it? Get what you need to make a start. Tackle one area at a time.

3. Which of the 10 tools for organizing time would be helpful to you? Decide on one of them. Buy what you need.

Success Principle

The successful woman takes control of her time and her environment.

For Additional Reading

Barnes, Emilie. *The Complete Holiday Organizer: A Busy Woman's Guide to Holiday Planning*. Harvest House.

————. *The Creative Home Organizer*. Harvest House.

————. *Daily Planner*. Harvest House, yearly.

————. *The 15-minute Organizer*. Harvest House.

————. *More House in My Day*. Harvest House.

————. *My Prayer Planner*. Harvest House.

————. *Survival for Busy Women: Establishing Efficient Home Management*. Harvest House.

Chapman, Annie, with Maureen Rank. *Smart Women Keep It Simple*. Bethany House.

Dillow, Linda. *Priority Planner*, revised and updated. Thomas Nelson.

CHAPTER TEN

A Patient Woman

IDENTIFY with Martha of Bethany, a woman who had more to do than she could possibly get done in one day. I think I understand how she felt that day when Mary visited with Jesus while she worked.

I imagine her thinking: *I should have had the meal on the table long ago. There's so much to do! I need help. Where's that sister of mine?*

I picture Martha, towel in her hands, frowning as she tries to get her sister's attention and she thinks: *Lazybones! How inconsiderate of her to sit here while I work! Why can't she be more like me: dependable, organized, hardworking, busy doing what must be done, accomplishing things? I wish she'd change! She'd sure be a lot easier to live with if she did!*

Mary, concentrating on the Master's words, doesn't notice. Impatient, Martha interrupts their conversation. "Master, don't You think it's rather unfair for me to do all the work while my sister sits here doing nothing? I'm fed up! I need help! Please tell her to come and help me."

Martha was impatient with the way her sister was, so she tried to change Mary through scolding, nagging, demanding, and confronting. How often in my impatience I try the same. Yet I do *not* want to be like Martha!

The Pharisees

The Pharisees had a problem with Mary as well. *Did you hear the latest about Mary? I can't believe how far she has gone! Why, she's nothing but a common slut, a prostitute. Disgusting! She ought to be punished for her behavior, bringing disgrace like that on the whole community. Maybe then she would be more like us—upright, correct, obedient to the law, respectable.*

The Pharisees, ever impatient with anyone not like themselves, set about to change the situation through naming, shaming, blaming, and punishing. I do *not* want to be like the Pharisees, but how often in my own impatience with others I have named, shamed, blamed, and sought to punish!

Judas Iscariot

Judas was another who was unhappy with Mary. I can imagine how he felt that day at Simon's feast when Mary broke her alabaster box. I can hear his impatient sigh. I can imagine him thinking: *I can't believe it! Spikenard! The most costly of perfumes! Why, that's equivalent to a whole year's wages! Incredible waste! Has she no sense as to the value of money? She should be more like me—shrewd, careful, a wise investor, intelligent, and a respected financier. She needs a little education in finances. Perhaps I should give it to her and to the rest of this motley group of Jesus' followers while I'm at it. They need to know that a penny saved is as good as one earned!*

I imagine that the banquet hall must have become very quiet as the people smelled the perfume and realized what Mary was doing. Judas took advantage of the quiet to make his statement. "I say there, to what purpose is this waste? If she had only given me the unbroken alabaster box, I could have sold it for a good profit. Imagine how many poor people we could have fed with it! Should we not be good stewards of the Lord's means?''

How terrible Mary must have felt as she listened to Judas' impatient words pointing out her errors, criticizing, arguing his case, lecturing on stewardship. I feel bad when I think how often I, in my own impatience, have done the same.

Playing God

Ron came home after a lengthy trip to find me upset about the actions of the three teenagers in our house. In fact, I was so impatient that I went to the train station to meet him, and before the poor man had his luggage in the car I had started my recital of woes. He listened to me all the way home. By the time he had unpacked, bathed, and eaten breakfast, I had told him all.

"Do you know what your problem is, Dorothy?" he asked.

My tears stopped. I looked at him in disbelief. "What? *My* problem? *I* don't have a problem, *they* have a problem! They need to be more . . .''

"Yes, Dorothy, *your* problem!" Ron chuckled. "You're trying to play God to those children. You're trying to make them over into your choleric, workaholic image. There's no way our children are going to turn into the serious, hardworking, always-do-what's-right, get-things-accomplished sort of person you are. They aren't made that way. So why don't you stop trying to change them?''

"Humph!" I grunted. "Maybe you're right.''

And the more I thought about it, the more I agreed with him. That's exactly what I had been trying to do, remake the children into my own image. How ridiculous when they were all so different!

David was our clown. He could make us laugh even when he was naughty. On his first day of school I told him, "You'd better be good, or you'll get a spanking from your teacher!''

He shook his head, rolled his big brown eyes, and said,

"Nobody will spank a nice little boy like me!" And no one did, though he deserved it more than once. David had a sanguine personality.

Esther was a quiet, thoughtful girl, but very, very slow. She was always the last one ready for anything, and this tried my patience no end. However, her room was always clean and tidy. Her drawers were organized, and the bottles on her dresser were arranged according to height. Esther had a melancholy, phlegmatic personality.

Stephen was a happy-go-lucky boy whose room was always a disaster area. He had lots of friends and was ready to go anywhere and try anything. He was generous, willing to share anything he had with friends. Stephen had a sanguine personality.

Ron was right! God created each of us as unique individuals. There was no need for me to become so impatient with those who did not have my particular temperament. Things went a lot better when I stopped trying to change my children and began instead to appreciate them for what special people they are.

Accepting People

I had to learn that just because other people are different from me doesn't make them wrong. The way we each approach life, our particular temperaments and personalities, has a lot to do with the way our DNA is lined up.

As Dr. David Lykken reports: "Much of what we think of as human individuality—temperament and pace and all the idiosyncrasies that make you different from your friends—may relate a lot more to your particular genetic individuality than we thought."

It takes a lot of pressure off when I realize that I am not responsible for the behavior of other people. It is liberating to realize that God created us as unique individuals, and I don't have to conform to someone else's image, but neither should I expect that person to conform to mine.

How Mary Changed

But still we have to admit that there are times when people do need to change. Mary needed to change, and she did change. But how did that change occur?

It was not by Martha's scolding, nagging, demanding, and confronting. It was not by the Pharisees' naming, shaming, blaming, and punishing. Neither was it because of Judas's criticizing, arguing, and educating.

Mary changed as she chose to yield to God's will. It came as the result of her own decision to allow God to transform the weaknesses of her personality into strengths for His cause. I cannot change another human being; only God has that power.

However, there are some things that I can do to facilitate that desire for change. For my model of facilitating change, I look to Christ.

Accept the Person

Jesus accepted Mary as she was. In response to Martha He said, ''Mary hath chosen that good part.'' In response to the Pharisees He commented, ''Neither do I condemn thee.'' In responding to Judas He affirmed, ''She hath wrought a good work upon me.''

Jesus accepted Mary as a total package, weaknesses as well as strengths. He loved her as a whole person, affirming her good points and overlooking past mistakes. He accepted her with unconditional love. It was in that total love and acceptance that Mary found the power that made her want to change.

Believe in the Person

Jesus' belief in Mary is expressed so well in *The Desire of Ages*: ''When to human eyes her case appeared hopeless, Christ saw in Mary capabilities for good. He saw the better traits of her character. The plan of redemption has invested humanity with great possibilities, and in Mary these possibilities were to be realized. Through His grace she became a partaker of the divine nature'' (p. 568).

Christ saw hope and beauty in Mary when she couldn't see these things in herself. He looked on the positive side of her character. He chose to talk about the good He saw. He believed that inside, Mary wanted to overcome her weaknesses and that given the opportunity she would choose to have Him supply the power. He did not get impatient with her, trying to force her to change. Instead, He believed in her.

Commit the Person to God

The third thing Jesus did to help Mary change was to commit her to God. We find this also in *The Desire of Ages*: "He might have extinguished every spark of hope in her soul, but He did not. It was He who had lifted her from despair and ruin. Seven times she had heard His rebuke of the demons that controlled her heart and mind. She had heard His strong cries to the Father in her behalf'' (*ibid.*).

Jesus prayed for Mary. He committed her into the hands of the only One who could give her the power to change.

Accept. Believe. Commit.

Accept. Believe. Commit. This is the ABC model Christ followed in facilitating change in Mary's life. It's one I can follow when I am tempted to become impatient with someone I love. It isn't an easy model to follow, but it is the only one that really works.

Joyce was raised an Adventist, but during her early 20s she drifted away from the church and married a non-Adventist she met at work. However, after her first child, Chelsea, was born, Joyce began to think about what she wanted for her little girl. She knew that included Sabbath school, so she began taking her each week. Joyce also got involved in a women's Bible study group and eventually decided to be rebaptized. Then she set out to convert her husband, Jake. He became angry.

"So now I'm not good enough for you?'' he sneered. "Well, I'll drink and smoke and party if I want to. Go to church if that makes you happy, but leave me out of it!''

For years Joyce tried to remake Jake into her image of a good Adventist husband and father. The more she scolded, nagged, and yelled, the further apart they grew. He began staying away in the evenings, leaving her alone with Chelsea . . . and her own fears.

Finally Joyce realized that she could not change Jake. Her way wasn't working. She decided just to love him and accept him—smoking, drinking, parties, and all. She would believe in him and pray for him, allowing God to work in His life.

Miracles began to happen. Jake met an Adventist man who shared his love of sports. An evangelist came to town, and Jake went at the invitation of his new friend. Bible studies followed, and Jake joined the church. It was a happy day for Joyce.

In telling me of her experience, Joyce commented, ''It wasn't until I stopped trying to change Jake that God was able to work. I'm so happy, but I know it's all God's doing and none of mine.''

The ABC Model Works

Virginia is another who knows that the ABC model for change works. Her husband was out of town and she was preparing to go to bed early when Becky stuck her head in her bedroom door. ''I need to talk to you,'' Becky said.

''Sure, honey,'' Virginia said, sitting down on the edge of the bed, motioning for her daughter to join her.

Becky started to cry. ''What's wrong, honey?'' Virginia asked, putting an arm around her daughter.

''You'll never love me again,'' Becky sobbed.

''You're my daughter.'' Virginia spoke firmly. ''No matter what you've done, I'll always love you. There's nothing you can do, no matter how bad, that would make me stop loving you.''

''But what about Daddy?'' The sobbing grew more intense. ''I know he'll never forgive me. I've ruined my life.''

"So you're pregnant," Virginia sighed.

"How did you know?" Becky's crying stopped.

"Mothers just know," Virginia answered, holding Becky tighter. Tears spilled down her own cheeks and wet Becky's hair. Just what she had feared had come to pass. "What are you going to do?" she asked at last.

"I want to keep the baby."

"Daddy and I will stand by you," Virginia said. "This doesn't make one speck of difference in our love for you. I think you've made the right decision. I'm proud of you!"

Becky had her baby, but long before it was born she stopped going to church. Guilt kept her away. She didn't want people whispering about her. She didn't think she'd be accepted.

Becky's life went from bad to worse, and she blamed God. There were lots of times Virginia felt like setting Becky straight, telling her a thing or two about whose fault it was, but she kept quiet. There were lots of things Becky needed to change, but Virginia knew that she couldn't make it happen for Becky.

Instead, she looked for ways to show Becky that she loved her. She looked for ways to encourage, to affirm the good things Becky was doing. That was easy because Becky was an excellent mother, a hard worker, and a thoughtful daughter.

Sometimes Virginia listened to Becky for hours, and often her only response was "We love you, honey. We believe in you. We are praying for you."

It was hard for Virginia to be patient as she watched Becky pursuing a lifestyle that she did not approve of, doing things she had raised her not to do. But she knew that preaching, scolding, blaming, and shaming would not help, so she did all that she could do—love her and pray for her.

God did work in Becky's life. She returned to Him and was rebaptized. At her baptism Becky testified, "I want to thank my mom and dad for standing by me. They never stopped loving me despite all the mistakes I've made. Without their love and prayers I wouldn't be here this morning. Thank you, Mom and Dad, for being so patient with me.''

Rate Yourself

Suppose the social committee in your church is planning a picnic that would include a softball game. What part would you like to play in the picnic? Where would you feel most comfortable performing?

1. Picnic coordinator. You are the one in charge. You call the shots and organize everyone else. You are the one with the whistle, calling everyone together for various activities. You might even be the umpire at the ball game.

2. Softball player. You want to be in the center of the action, whether it is the baseball game or a tug-of-war. You like to hear the cheers of the crowd as you come in for a home run or pull the knot across the line.

3. Food committee. Or any other committee, for that matter. You like to work behind the scenes, attending to necessary details that make the picnic a success. You are pleased to prepare food, make posters, send out invitations, buy supplies, or go ahead of time to lay out an obstacle course.

4. Cheering section. You bring your lawn chair or blanket and are content to sit in the background and watch the others work and perform. You are part of the cheering crowd, enjoying yourself most as you sit back and relax for the afternoon. If you do participate in games, it is because others urge you, and you do it just to please them and not make a scene.

Which number best describes you—1, 2, 3, 4?

1. If you chose picnic coordinator, you are likely a choleric personality. You like to get things done . . . now! You are energetic, dynamic, hardworking, disciplined, and well organized. You don't mind telling other people what to do. A sense of being in control of a situation is very important to you.

2. If you picked baseball player, you probably have a more sanguine personality. You like people, action, and the limelight. You like people to cheer you and laugh at your jokes. Being around other people energizes you. Having lots of friends is very important to you.

3. If you chose food committee, you are likely a melancholy personality who enjoys attending to details. You want things done right and are happy to do background chores to make a program a success. When it is all over, someone with a melancholy temperament will probably write it up for the church newsletter.

4. If you settled on cheering section, you probably have a phlegmatic temperament. You would rather be in the audience, sit back, relax, and enjoy the experience from the sidelines. You are steady and dependable and easy to get along with.

· **Personal Growth Exercises**

1. If you have never taken a temperament test, contact your conference women's ministry director or family life director. One of them may be able to give you a test or tell you about a coming seminar on the temperaments.

2. Read *Your Personality Tree*, by Florence Littauer. It goes into temperament types in detail. In the back of the book you will also find a helpful personality inventory.

3. Other books that may be of interest to you are: *Why Can't My Mate Be More Like Me?* by Len McMillan; *One of a Kind: Making the Most of Your Child's Uniqueness*, by LaVonne Neff; and *Please Understand Me!* by David Keirsey and Marilyn Bates.

Success Principle

The most successful way to facilitate change in others is to accept them, believe in them, and commit them to God.

For Additional Reading

Keirsey, David and Bates, Marilyn. *Please Understand Me*. Prometheus Nemesis Books.

Littaur, Florence. *Your Personality Tree.*

McMillan, Len. *Why Can't My Mate Be More Like Me?* Pacific Press Publishing Association.

Neff, LaVonne. *One of a Kind: Making the Most of Your Child's Uniqueness.*

Stoop, David and Stoop, Jan. *The Intimacy Factor.* Nelson. (Discusses temperaments based on the Myers-Briggs system and their affect on relationships.)

CHAPTER ELEVEN

A Victorious Woman

COLES ROAD in Bangalore, India, is a busy street in a residential area. The spreading branches of flowering trees make it a pleasant place to walk despite the heavy traffic.

Auto rickshas, buses, horse-drawn carts, motor scooters, cars, and cycles crowd the road. Cows, dogs, and people wander on the dusty paths between the street and compound walls. Street vendors carrying baskets of flowers, eggs, and vegetables on their heads shout their wares at each gate.

In spite of the congestion, the street is remarkably clean, swept each morning by hand, the piles of rubbish gathered in baskets and dumped into concrete dust bins placed in every block.

Walking down this street one October afternoon, I heard a weak meow above the noise of the traffic. I stopped a moment, trying to locate the owner of that pathetic voice.

"Meow!" There it was just a few feet ahead of me. Beside an overflowing dust bin I saw a tiny kitten lying on a banana leaf. I knelt down and patted the kitten's matted fur. Her eyes were sealed shut with pus, but at my touch I could feel her begin to purr. I picked her up. She weighed almost nothing and was so small she fit comfortably into the cup of one hand.

"Oh, you poor, poor thing!" I said. "Did someone throw you out here to die? I'll take you home with me."

For several days I fussed over that stray kitten, trying to get her to eat, cleaning her, dressing her wounds. I made her a bed in a basket beside my bed and cared for her day and night.

I cried all afternoon the day she died. I had tried so hard, but I had failed. That evening I wrote a poem I entitled "Failure." The last verse says:

> The cry is gone. Pussy is dead.
> All my care has been in vain.
> Oh, God, why? I have done my best.
> Nothing is left—but the pain.

My reaction to my failure to save a stray cat may seem overdone unless you know the struggles I was going through at that time. It seemed to me in those moments that I was not only a failure as a rescuer of kittens but a failure as a mother, a failure as a wife, a failure as a missionary, and a failure as a Christian.

From the perspective of 17 years later, things look quite different. I can see how God has brought good out of each trial, success out of each failure, and victory from each defeat.

It is easy now to see the good that came out of that difficult period of my life: the incentive to write my first book, the beginning of Sunshine Children's Home for abandoned children, lessons of dependence upon God, the power of prayer, and the strength of love. It was not so easy to see then.

The Flip Side of Failure

"Success is the flip side of failure," the conference publishing department director used to tell us student colporteurs. He kept insisting that "success is failure turned inside out, the silver tint to the clouds of doubt."

When I had a bad day canvassing, I could hear him saying enthusiastically, "Don't give up! Learn from each failure, and you will have success. God has not called you to failure, but to success. When the going gets tough, the tough get going."

My mother had another way of saying the same thing. "If at first you don't succeed, try, try again. 'Tis a lesson all should heed, try, try again."

I remember her reciting that proverb as she handed me back a skirt I was trying to make. The seam was crooked, the hem uneven, and the waistband wasn't put on correctly.

"Rip it out," she said. "It's all wrong."

"I don't want to do it over," I pouted.

"Do it anyway," Mother insisted. "Anything worth doing is worth doing well. If at first you don't succeed, try, try again."

I started to cry. The task seemed enormous.

"There's no shame in failing," Mother said quietly. "The shame is in not learning from your failures."

I did it over, and with Mother's expert help turned that failure into a success, a skirt that I was proud to wear!

What to Do With Failure

There are six things we can do with failure: acknowledge it; thank God for it; learn from it; use it as a stepping-stone to success; overcome it; or transform it into an opportunity.

1. Acknowledge it. Stop trying to excuse it. Because of sin all human beings experience failure. We fool no one when we pretend to be perfect. Confession of our failures allows for the grace of forgiveness and the opportunity for change.

2. Thank God for it. "The humiliation of defeat often proves a blessing by showing us our inability to do the will of God without His aid" (Ellen G. White, *Patriarchs and Prophets,* p. 633).

Not so long ago I learned this lesson when faced with a particularly difficult teaching situation. I used every trick I had up my sleeve after 15 years in the classroom. Nothing worked.

I felt like an utter failure as a teacher. It was then that I laid the problem before the Lord and said, "I have no more ideas. I feel like giving up. All my plans have failed."

Looking back to the night of my despair, I can thank God for allowing me to reach that point, for it was only then that He was able to take control. When the successful year was finished I could say only, "Thank You, Lord, for the miracle You wrought!"

3. *Learn from it*. "Reverses will teach caution. We learn by the things we suffer. Thus we gain experience" (Ellen G. White, *Gospel Workers*, p. 492). "We are to learn from past experience how to avoid failure" (Ellen G. White, *Testimonies*, vol. 7, p. 239).

Often when I do something really dumb, my husband says to me, "Charge it to tuition." His acceptance and forgiveness of my failures have had a lot to do with any successes I have had.

The rejection of a manuscript is difficult for me to handle. The first time I had a book manuscript returned I hid it in the back of a file drawer and didn't look at it for a year. Then I got it out, tried to learn how I could improve it, redid the manuscript, and sent it back. Again it was rejected!

I was devastated. I felt a failure as an author. Again I hid it for a year but eventually got it out and tried to learn where I'd gone wrong. I corrected those mistakes and sent it off again. This time it was accepted for publication. I learned much from those rejections.

4. *Use it as a stepping-stone to success*. "Some God trains by bringing to them disappointment and apparent failure. It is His purpose that they shall learn to master difficulties. He inspires them with a determination to prove every apparent failure a success. Often men pray and weep because of the perplexities and obstacles that confront them. But if they will hold the beginning of their confidence steadfast unto the end, God will make their way clear. Success will come as they struggle against apparently insurmountable

difficulties'' (*Gospel Workers*, p. 269).

When we received our call to India I wrote to the brethren, informing them that I was a teacher and asking them what they planned for me to do.

A letter came back. "We expect nothing of you but to make your husband happy."

, That sounded easy enough to do. No need, then, to take my teaching materials. It would only mean extra baggage. I threw away or gave away all my teaching materials.

I was not yet off the boat in Madras harbor when I was informed, "We have a job for you, Dorothy. We'd like you to teach the dozen or so expatriate children."

We had almost no textbooks, and it took more than six months for them to arrive by surface mail. Meanwhile that apparent perplexity turned into a real blessing, for it caused me to do some of the most creative teaching of my career. That experience literally transformed the way I teach. We took field trips into the community, learned to do research in *World Book Encyclopedia,* and wrote our own reading materials for first grade. The children did much more writing and exploring than they would have done with textbooks. We had a wonderful time!

Having once escaped from the tyranny of the textbook, I have never been so tied to it since. Because of a situation that seemed to promise failure, I became a better teacher than I would have been otherwise. While struggling against failure, it became a stepping-stone to success.

5. Overcome it. All failure is not sin, but all sin is failure. If sin is our problem, then we can by the grace of God overcome that failure. Jesus came to earth not only to die for our moral failures but to show us how to overcome them. The methods He has given us are Scripture, the Holy Spirit, prayer, song, and the ministry of angels.

When tempted by the devil in the wilderness, Jesus fought failure with Scripture. "It is written," He said, quoting verses He had learned at His mother's knee. "Thy word have I hid in my heart," said David, "that I might not sin against thee."

Jesus has given us the Holy Spirit to help us "in the battle against sin" (Ellen G. White, *The Acts of the Apostles,* p. 56) and to keep "evil under the control of the conscience" (*The SDA Bible Commentary*, Ellen G. White Comments, vol. 6, p. 1112).

Angels are another source of help. "When unconsciously we are in danger of exerting a wrong influence, the angels will be by our side, prompting us to a better course, choosing our words for us, and influencing our actions" (Ellen G. White, *Christ's Object Lessons*, p. 341).

Prayer is indispensable in obtaining victory over sin. "True prayer takes hold upon Omnipotence and gives us the victory. Upon his knees the Christian obtains strength to resist temptation" (*Testimonies,* vol. 4, p. 616). We are also told that "the darkness of the evil one encloses those who neglect to pray" (Ellen G. White, *Steps to Christ,* p. 94).

Have you ever thought of singing as a means of overcoming sin? It is one of the methods Jesus used while on earth (*Education*, p. 166), and it is a powerful tool for Adventist women today (*ibid.*, p. 168).

6. *Transform it*. It is possible to turn a defeat into victory. Sometimes all that is necessary is just a change of the way we look at things. The successful Adventist woman will see a possibility in every failure. She will seek, by God's power, to transform that failure into success.

The story of Brett Livingstone Strong and the Malibu Rock is an excellent illustration of seeing the possibility in failure and transforming it into success.

A 116-ton rock perched above the Pacific Coast Highway in Malibu, California, and threatened those who lived below. Removal of the rock took four days and cost the government close to $1 million.

Brett Strong looked at that worthless failure of a rock and saw in it something of great value. He purchased it for $100, then paid $25,000 to move it to a grassy knoll near a shopping center 20 miles away. For the next 70 days he worked to transform that rock.

When he was finished he had created a remarkable likeness of John Wayne, which was purchased by a man in Scottsdale, Arizona, for $1 million. Brett Strong took a million-dollar failure and transformed it into a million-dollar success.

By God's grace and power that's what I want to do with the failures of my life.

Rate Yourself

On a scale of 1 to 5, rate yourself in the way you deal with failure and disappointment. Five is the best.

1. I take full responsibility for my mistakes. I acknowledge my failures and confess my sins.

1   2   3   4   5

2. I am able to learn from my failures.

1   2   3   4   5

3. I consistently thank God for my disappointments and failures.

1   2   3   4   5

4. I use each failure as a stepping-stone to success.

1   2   3   4   5

5. I am using all the agencies God has provided to overcome sin in my life.

1   2   3   4   5

6. I have transformed each failure of my life into an opportunity.

1   2   3   4   5

Personal Growth Exercises

1. Divide a sheet of paper into two columns. In the first

column make a list of some of the major failures or disappointments of your life. In the second column write down at least one thing you have learned from each experience.

2. Look up the following texts. What does each one tell you about what to do with failure? Jude 24; 1 John 1:9; Phil. 4:13; 3:13, 14; Prov. 28:13; 1 Cor. 15:57; Isa. 61:3; Rom. 8:28.

3. "As the world's Redeemer, Christ was constantly confronted with apparent failure," says Ellen White. How did He deal with these discouraging circumstances? Read pages 678, 679 of *The Desire of Ages*. Find four ways Jesus dealt with failure.

4. Collect biographies of people who have taken failure and turned it into an opportunity for success. An example is *Think Big*, by Dr. Ben Carson.

Success Principle

With God's help every failure can become a stepping-stone to success.

For Additional Reading

Briscoe, Jill. *Women Who Changed Their World*. Victor Books.

Carson, Ben. *Gifted Hands*. Review and Herald Publishing Association.

_____. *Think Big*. Review and Herald Publishing Association.

CHAPTER TWELVE

A Courageous Woman

ABY KYLE arrived two months early. Shortly after his birth he stopped breathing. An alert nurse brought him around. During the next week the staff revived him a dozen times. After three months Sharon and Trevor took their son home with the knowledge that there was likely brain damage. Today Kyle goes to school in a wheelchair. Through therapy he's learning to cope with cerebral palsy.

"You need to have another child for Kyle's sake," the doctor told Sharon when Kyle was 4 years old.

"No," Sharon shook her head. "I would be afraid to risk it happening again."

"And what if it did?" the doctor replied. "You and Trevor are doing a beautiful job with Kyle. You could handle it. However, the risk is minimal. The chances are one in a million."

"But it's that millionth chance I'm afraid of," said Sharon.

"Life is full of risks," the doctor answered. "Every time you cross the street you take a risk. What if you said, 'I might get hit by a car, so I won't cross the street'? You'd never get anywhere. You've got to take some risks in life.''

At times I feel a little like Sharon, afraid to venture out into something new, afraid to take a risk. I know I am not alone in my fears. What holds us back from achieving a lifetime dream? What keeps us from boldly stepping out to claim success? Why don't we have the courage to be all that we can be?

Fear Holds Us Back

What are we afraid of? Embarrassment, pain, and the unknown. We're afraid of what people might say, or worried about losing a relationship. We're scared of making a mistake, of failing.

It takes courage to rise above these fears, to walk boldly on in spite of the fear in our hearts. Dorothy Bernard defines courage as ''fear that has said its prayers.'' General George Patton suggests that courage is simply ''fear holding on a minute longer.'' Courage is an act of the will—a choice on our part to go on, to take a risk regardless of our fear.

Successful Women Are Risk Takers

Every successful woman since time began has been willing to risk failure that she might gain success.

My list of courageous women includes intrepid pioneer missionary Narcissa Whitman and the dauntless Anne Judson. Fearless Mary Slessor of Calabar is there, and so is brave Harriet Tubman. I would include the valiant Elizabeth Fry as well as spunky Florence Nightingale. My list includes stalwart Catherine Booth and the daring Amelia Earhart.

These are all women who could have chosen to travel life's main highway, where they would be comfortable and safe. Instead, they chose to hike a new trail. The path they traveled was uncomfortable at times, risky and unpredictable. Their way was uncertain, uncharted, but the scenery, exciting!

I want to be a woman who travels new trails, a courageous woman such as Ana Stahl or Ida Scudder. I aspire to be a woman who dares to stand up for principle, a woman such as Anne Hutchinson or Ellen White. I want to be a woman unafraid of using her talents, a woman such as Wilma Rudolph or Marian Anderson. I'd like to be a woman able to risk succeeding despite handicaps, a woman such as Joni Eareckson Tada or Carla Mae Salvail.

Carla's Story

Twenty-two-year-old Carla Mae Salvail has had more than her share of pain. Three years ago her husband of one year died of meningitis. She began working two jobs to earn money to finish her education at Simon Fraser University in Vancouver, British Columbia.

After eight months of 24-hour workdays, Carla was exhausted, pushing herself beyond limits in her grief. On the way home from work one night she skidded on a wet bridge, hit a pole, and tore the car in half. Having suffered multiple injuries, she lay in a coma for 28 days.

Today she's confined to a wheelchair, unable to talk. One hand is useless. With the other she pecks out messages on a laptop computer. She spends two hours a day in physical therapy, doing leg pushes and standing in her walker.

"Walking, I hope, by two years," she types, smiling. On her desk are university textbooks in political science and psychology. This past term she scored two A-pluses and managed a 3.15 grade point average. Her goal is to be a psychologist for the deaf. She's teaching herself sign language.

In 1992 Carla won the Terry Fox medal for "someone who has demonstrated those personal qualities of courage in adversity, and dedication to society, which have been exemplified by Terry Fox."

I See Courage

Courage is demonstrated in many ways. I see it in the face of my friend who is winning in her fight with cancer. I see it in the eyes of another who struggles to carry on after the death of her companion of 40 years. I find it in the forgiveness of a friend whose husband was unfaithful. I see it in the devotion of a woman pastor I know as she obeys God's call to the ministry in spite of prejudice. I see it in another friend who is trying single-handedly to raise three children and still keep food on the table.

Courage is asking for ginger ale when everyone else is having beer. It is sending a manuscript off to a publisher or giving a public testimony for the first time. It is becoming a refugee for the sake of a child or choosing to give 110 percent to make a marriage work.

Courage is seeking counsel to overcome the abuse of childhood, and sometimes it is walking out of a destructive relationship. It is daring to reach out to neighbors with God's love, and it is refusing to be a codependent for an alcoholic husband.

Courage is saying no to the good in order to say yes to the best. It is refusing to believe gossip about a friend, and it is confronting someone who has wronged you. It is going back to school after the children have grown up. It is showing kindness to an enemy or daring to be honest with a friend.

How to Have Courage

It's easy to say "Have courage!" But how do you do it? What strategies will help me increase my courage quotient? My study has led me to four practical things I can do.

1. Talk courage. In his book *The Psychology of Winning* Dr. Denis Waitley says: "Current research on the effect of words and images on the functions of the body offers amazing evidence of the power that words, spoken at random, can have on body functions monitored on biofeedback equipment. Since thoughts can raise and lower body temperature, secrete hormones, relax muscles and nerve endings, dilate and constrict arteries, and raise and lower pulse rate—it is obvious that we need to control the language we use on ourselves."

Eighty years before this amazing research, Ellen White stated: "Open your heart to the bright beams of the Sun of Righteousness, and let not one breath of doubt, one word of unbelief, escape your lips, lest you sow the seeds of doubt. . . . I entreat you to have courage in the Lord. Divine strength is ours; and let us talk courage and strength and faith" (*Testimonies to Ministers*, p. 391).

Richard C. Foster confirms this principle in his book *Celebration of Discipline*: "It is not even important that the person believe what he or she is repeating, only that it be repeated. The inner mind is thus trained and will eventually respond by modifying behavior to conform to the affirmation" (p. 65).

Just after the great disappointment of October 22, 1844, a number of the early Adventists were gathered in a meeting. Some were weeping; all were looking downcast and sad.

Suddenly a newcomer entered the room and seeing the glum faces and slumped shoulders, he shouted, "Courage in the Lord, brethren; courage in the Lord!"

The saddened men and women looked up in surprise. Didn't he know what they had been through?

"Courage in the Lord, brethren!" he repeated, smiling broadly. "Courage in the Lord!" Here and there he found an answering smile, and a feeble "Praise the Lord." He kept repeating "Courage in the Lord!" until "every face was aglow, and every voice lifted in praise to God" (Ellen G. White, *Gospel Workers*, p. 265).

2. *Praise God*. "If more praising of God were engaged in now, hope and courage and faith would steadily increase" (Ellen G. White, *Prophets and Kings*, p. 202).

Vibia Perpetua of Carthage, North Africa, a martyr of the third century, is an example of the power of praise. She was condemned to be thrown into the arena among wild animals and then to be killed by a gladiator's sword.

Perpetua nursed her infant son until just before her execution. Then she walked to the arena, her face radiant, singing a psalm. She was thrown in with a wild steer.

She was gored by the steer but felt no pain. So terrible was the sight that the crowd roared, "Enough! Enough!" As the animal was led away, Perpetua called for her brother and begged him to remain true to the faith. Then she bravely turned to face the gladiator. When he gave her but a slight wound, she guided his sword to her throat and died, still praising God. What courage!

3. Have faith in God's promises. "It was Caleb's faith in God that gave him courage" (Ellen G. White, *Testimonies*, vol. 5, p. 378).

In relating the story of Elijah after Mount Carmel, Ellen White talks about the need for hope and courage. "These," she says, "are the fruit of faith." She continues, "Have faith in God. He knows your need. He has all power. His infinite love and compassion never weary. Fear not that He will fail of fulfilling His promise" (*Prophets and Kings,* pp. 164, 165).

My first testing of God's promise of courage came during my freshman year at Mount Vernon Academy when I was faced with my first piano recital. I was terrified of performing in public. During the Sunday afternoon practice my knees shook, my hands trembled, and my mind went blank. I made so many mistakes that I started to cry. "I can't do it," I told my teacher. "I'm too scared. I'll make a fool of myself tonight."

"I know that you can do it with God's help," she replied. "He'll give you the courage you need."

"I don't think so," I whimpered.

"Go to your room and look up Philippians 4:13," she suggested. "That's a promise from God to you. Ask Him to keep it. You'll do fine tonight!"

Back at my room I read, "I can do all things through Christ which strengtheneth me." Courage did come as I asked God for it. I got through the recital without embarrassment.

4. Accept the gift of the Holy Spirit. "Oh, how precious is the sweet influence of the Spirit of God as it comes to depressed or despairing souls, encouraging the fainthearted, strengthening the feeble, and imparting courage and help to the tried servants of the Lord!'' (*Patriarchs and Prophets*, p. 657).

Beverly LaHaye knows that this is true. Although a pastor's wife, she was a fearful, introverted person, afraid to speak in public, anxious about entertaining, worried about what people thought of her and her children.

Then one day at a church retreat she quietly knelt and surrendered her life to God. She said, "Lord, fill me with Your Holy Spirit. Take away my spirit of fear, and give me in its place the spirit 'of power, of love, and of a sound mind.' Do the impossible in my life.''

In relating the experience she says: "There was no outward sign or expression except for a beautiful, quiet peace that settled in my heart and the new confidence that God was going to do something far better with my life than I had been able to do" (Beverly LaHaye, *The Spirit-Controlled Woman*, p. 14).

Her husband, Tim LaHaye, testifies, "I have witnessed a sweet, soft-spirited worry machine that was afraid of her own shadow become transformed into a gracious, outgoing, radiant woman whom God has used to inspire thousands of women to accept Him and the abundant life He offers" (*ibid.*, p. 8).

I believe that God is just as willing to gift me with courage! By His grace and power I too can become a courageous woman!

Rate Yourself

Check the areas of your life in which you feel a need for courage at the present time.

__Marriage	__Health	__Career
__Children	__Relationships	__Addictions
__Finances	__Church work	__Witnessing
__Parents	__Talents	__Temptation

___Trials   ___Recreation   ___Habits
___Conflict   ___Grieving   ___Principles
___Future   ___Dreams   ___Education

Practicing Success Principles

1. All of us face small risks every day, things that we are afraid to do. Which of the following are risks for you? Speaking in public? Meeting a stranger? Asking for something? Offering advice? Making a phone call? Praying in public? Arguing a grade? Interviewing for a job? Learning a new skill? Sending off a manuscript? Standing up for a friend who is being gossiped about? Telling someone to go to the end of the line?

2. Decide to take at least one small risk every day for a week. Ask God to help you do what is difficult for you. Claim the following promises to give you courage: Phil. 4:19; Isa. 41:10; Joshua 1:9; Ps. 27:1.

3. Read "Call to Travel" in *Life Sketches*, by Ellen G. White. Note how afraid she was to risk telling her experience as the Lord had instructed her.

Success Principle

The courageous woman follows The Giraffe Principle: You have to stick your neck out if you want to reach your goal!

For Additional Reading

Curtis, June. *The Courage of a Woman*. Harvest House.
Foster, Richard C. *Celebration of Discipline*.
Waitley, Dennis. *The Psychology of Winning*.

Other Helpful Reading

Bacher, June Masters. *The Quiet Heart: A Daily Devotional*. Harvest House.
_____. *Quiet Moments for Women: A Daily Devotional*. Harvest House.
Barnes, Emilie. *The Spirit of Loveliness*. Harvest House.

Beardsley, Lou, and Toni Spry. *The Fulfilled Woman*. Harvest House.

Houtz, Elsa. *The Working Mother's Guide to Sanity*. Harvest House.

Joy, Donald. *Bonding: Relationships in the Image of God*. Word.

Lenzkes, Susan. *Everybody's Breaking Pieces Off of Me: Stress-relieving Devotions for Women*. Thomas Nelson.

Mills, Kathi. *Mommy, Where Are You? Investing in the Lives of Your Children*. Harvest House.

Neal, C. W. *Your 30-Day Journey to Becoming a Great Wife*. Thomas Nelson.

Otis, Rose, editor. *Among Friends*. Review and Herald Publishing Association.

Otto, Donna. *The Stay-at-home Mom*. Harvest House.

Pippert, Rebecca Manley. *Out of the Saltshaker, Into the World*. Inter-Varsity.

Shropshire, Marie. *In Touch with God*. Harvest House.

Improve Your Prayer Life

My Prayer Notebook
Developed by Nancy Van Pelt, this creative approach to personal prayer gives you a way to record your prayer requests and answers. It will deepen your faith as you see evidence of God's leading and make your prayer time more effective as you focus on specific types of requests each day of the week. Includes lightly lined record sheets and dividers. Refill sheets available. Loose-leaf notebook, US$18.95, Cdn$25.60.

Practical Pointers to Personal Prayer
Drawing from personal experience, Carrol Johnson Shewmake leads you to a more meaningful, power-filled prayer life. Paper, 128 pages. US$7.95, Cdn$10.75.

Sanctuary Secrets to Personal Prayer
Join Carrol Johnson Shewmake in a unique prayer experience that takes you through the steps performed by the priests in the Old Testament sanctuary. Paper, 92 pages, US$6.95, Cdn$9.40.

Incredible Answers to Prayer
This exciting collection of stories about answered prayer will make you rejoice that you too serve the "Lord of the impossible." By Roger Morneau. Paper, 96 pages. US$6.95, Cdn$9.40.

More Incredible Answers to Prayer
Roger Morneau shares stories of how God has worked in surprising ways in response to intercessory prayer. He answers questions about intercessory prayer, discusses preventive prayer, and explains how to preserve a vital relationship with God. Paper, 96 pages. US$7.95, Cdn$10.75.

To order, call **1-800-765-6955** or write to ABC Mailing Service, P.O. Box 1119, Hagerstown, MD 21741. Send check or money order. Enclose applicable sales tax and 15 percent (minimum US$2.50) for postage and handling. Prices and availability subject to change without notice. Add GST in Canada.

Daily Devotionals for Women

Among Friends
This daily devotional draws together the wisdom and creativity of more than 150 Adventist women from around the world. Representing all walks of life, they open their hearts, sharing thoughts, feelings, and ideas about things that matter most to them. They speak candidly about their problems and worries. They rejoice at evidences of God's love. Join this celebration of friendship among women who love the Lord and enjoy the spiritual refreshment and fellowship these devotionals bring. Hardcover with dust jacket, 432 pages. US$14.95, Cdn$18.70.

The Listening Heart
In these trying "end-times," when a day can bring more pressure than pleasure, you'll be inspired by the very personal experiences of more than 150 women who share from their hearts. They tell how God has sustained them through a wide variety of experiences, and how they are learning to listen to His still, small voice. Their stories will help focus your thoughts, orient your day, and lead you to the Source of peace. Hardcover with dust jacket, US$14.95, Cdn$18.70. A matching journal is available.

To order, call **1-800-765-6955** or write to ABC Mailing Service, P.O. Box 1119, Hagerstown, MD 21741. Send check or money order. Enclose applicable sales tax and 15 percent (minimum US$2.50) for postage and handling. Prices and availability subject to change without notice. Add GST in Canada.

Inspirational Reading

His Guiding Hand
In these short inspirational stories Dorothy Davenport shares her own personal answers to prayer. Learn how miracles saved her and her family from certain death, allowed her to demonstrate Jesus' love to hurting people, and provided direction in times of need. Here is strong assurance that no problem we face is too great for God to handle. Paper, 96 pages. US$7.95, Cdn$10.75.

A Warm and Welcome Place
Come. A rare treat awaits you in these writings by June Strong. Filled with countless treasures, they bid you escape your hectic schedule and enter a warm and welcome place to enjoy the company of God and the simple pleasures that He offers. In each reading the commonplace bursts with new meaning. From a sunbeam piercing the blackness of a storm, a glass shattered by an exuberant child, and an old gander named Charlie who can't fly come fresh insights into God's love. Whether you join the author for quiet reflection in her prayer garden or step inside the old farmhouse bustling with family and friends, the warm and welcome place she takes you is always near the heart of God. Paper, 159 pages. US$8.95, Cdn$12.10.

To order, call **1-800-765-6955** or write to ABC Mailing Service, P.O. Box 1119, Hagerstown, MD 21741. Send check or money order. Enclose applicable sales tax and 15 percent (minimum US$2.50) for postage and handling. Prices and availability subject to change without notice. Add GST in Canada.

By Ben Carson

Gifted Hands
Medical breakthroughs have brought this Adventist physician worldwide acclaim. But as the media flock to him for interviews, he gives the glory to God. This fascinating autobiography reveals the tremendous challenges and obstacles God helped him overcome. By Ben Carson, M.D., with Cecil Murphey. Paper, 232 pages. US$9.95, Cdn$13.45.

Also available, *Gifted Hands Video*, US$19.95, Cdn$29.60, and *Gifted Hands Audio Pages* (two 60-minute cassettes read by Dr. Carson), US$12.95, Cdn$19.25.

Think Big
Dr. Carson shares the Think Big philosophy that changed him from a street-smart ghetto kid with bad grades and a bad attitude into one of the most celebrated pediatric neurosurgeons in the world. This motivational book shows you how to succeed no matter what your circumstances. Hardcover, 256 pages. US$14.95, Cdn$20.20.

Think Big Audio Pages
A condensed presentation of *Think Big*, read by Dr. Ben Carson. Two 60-minute cassettes. US$12.95, Cdn$19.25.

To order, call **1-800-765-6955** or write to ABC Mailing Service, P.O. Box 1119, Hagerstown, MD 21741. Send check or money order. Enclose applicable sales tax and 15 percent (minimum US$2.50) for postage and handling. Prices and availability subject to change without notice. Add GST in Canada.